HOW TO SPEAK
MIDWESTERN

Edward McClelland

First edition 2016

ISBN: 978-0-9977742-7-6

Belt Publishing
1667 E. 40th Street #1G1
Cleveland, Ohio 44120

www.beltmag.com

Book design by Meredith Pangrace
Cover by David Wilson

To my favorite Mitches, Kolhoff and Gerber:
one will never leave the Midwest, and one will never stop
wishing he could move back.

HOW TO SPEAK
MIDWESTERN

TABLE OF CONTENTS

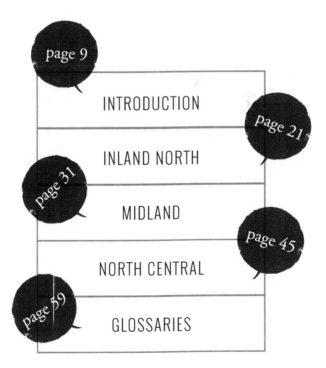

 **INTRODUCTION**

I first found out I had an accent when I was a sophomore at the University of Michigan. I was taking a class in linguistics, and I asked a student from New Jersey whether she'd noticed anything distinctive about the way I and other Michiganders talk.

"You say 'cayen' for 'can'," she told me without delay.

When I brought this up in class, the professor drew an æ on the blackboard to symbolize the phonetic phenomenon known as "*a* raising." As I later learned, this is a feature of the Northern Cities Vowel Shift, which also causes speakers in the Great Lakes region to call a box a "bahhx" and pronounce the number seven as "suvun"—pronunciations that distinguish our voices from the rest of the English-speaking world.

Accents are an important element of regional identity. And an important element of Midwestern identity is believing you don't have an accent—that you speak a neutral brand of standardized English from which all other Americans deviate. When linguist Matthew Gordon was researching his doctoral thesis on the Northern Cities Vowel Shift at the University of Michigan, his subjects were perplexed by his interest in their accents, because, of course, there's absolutely nothing exotic about Midwestern speech.

"It's part of the reputation the Midwest has of being the standard," Gordon says. "I think that that ideology—this is standard English, this is the English that broadcasters use—kind of leads people to not hear how different their speech is until they travel outside the area. At the University of Michigan, when you talk to students in linguistics class, one of the questions they ask you is 'Why don't we have an accent?'"

Every part of the United States has its own accent. The Midwest—defined, for the purposes of this book, as west of Exit 41 on the New York State Thruway, east of the Missouri River, and north of the Ohio River—has three distinct dialect regions, each formed by nineteenth-century migratory patterns. The Inland North—the lower Great Lakes from Buffalo to Milwaukee—was settled by Yankees from western New England who imported their flat, nasal speech to the Midwest. The Midland, which stretches from western Pennsylvania in a belt across Ohio, Indiana, Illinois, and Iowa, coincides with the westward route of Scots-Irish who arrived in this country through Philadelphia and Baltimore, bringing with them such still-in-use terms as "jag" for thorn and "run" for creek. The North Central encompasses Upper Michigan, Wisconsin, and Minnesota, destinations for Germans and Scandinavians who transposed pronunciations and grammatical features from their native languages onto English. If you've ever heard an Iron Ranger from Minnesota say "Let's go Dulut'," you've heard the lack of prepositions or a *th* sound that mark Finnish at work in English.

With so much linguistic diversity in our own region, why do Midwesterners believe we speak an unaccented English? The answer goes back to the early twentieth century, and the dawn of broadcasting. At the time, Midwestern speech was not the default, or even the most prestigious, way of speaking American English. The Transatlantic Accent associated with upper-class northeasterners such as President Franklin D. Roosevelt, actress Katharine Hepburn, and, later, author George Plimpton, was a British-influenced manner of speaking popular with politicians and film stars. It was considered so sophisticated that even Ohio-bred president William McKinley used it in his public speeches, telling his fellow citizens that "recent events have imposed upon the patriotic people of this country a responsibility and duty greatah than that of any since the Civil Waugh." But Transatlantic English was artificial, affected, and associated with a social class that would lose credibility during the Great Depression.

In the 1920s, the industrial Midwest wielded far more political, cultural, and economic influence that it does today. Between Ulysses S. Grant and Warren G. Harding, seven of the nine presidents who entered the White House by election were from Ohio. Cleveland billed itself as "the best location in the nation," because it was situated within 500 miles of half the North American population—a claim no longer true, now that so many Midwesterners have moved to the Sun Belt. The steel mills and auto plants drew millions of Southern and Eastern European immigrants who adopted Inland North as their dialect model. Perhaps most importantly, the nation's leading pronunciation expert was John S. Kenyon, a philologist at Ohio's Hiram College, which is just east of Cleveland. Kenyon was the author of two books, *American Pronunciation* (1924) and *A Pronouncing Dictionary of American English* (1944), and was pronunciation editor of *Webster's New International Dictionary of the English Language*. In these roles, Kenyon championed rhoticity, the pronunciation of *r*'s wherever they appear in words: he preferred "war" to the Transatlantic "waugh." Kenyon also favored pronouncing "not" like "naht," instead of "nawt." These were both features of the Inland North speech he heard in northeastern Ohio.

Kenyon's pronunciation standards influenced James F. Bender, author of the *NBC Handbook of Pronunciation*. The most oft-heard newscasters of the World War II era—Lowell Thomas, H.V. Kaltenborn, and Edward R. Murrow—pronounced all their *r*'s, as Kenyon would have advised.

After World War II, non-rhoticity—the dropping of *r*'s—fell completely out of favor with Middle America. Katharine Hepburn asked her leading men, "Ahh you coming, deah?" but Doris Day, a native of Cincinnati, asked, "Are you coming, dear?" An increasingly middle-class society had no use for posh upper-class accents.

At the same time, in a further blow to non-rhoticity, lower-class New Yorkers became stigmatized in popular culture as clownish wiseacres—Bugs Bunny, the Bowery Boys—or thuggish gangsters. And Southerners, of course, were uneducated bigots whose *r*-less drawls were associated with racist sheriffs and senators. Some of the late twentieth century's most popular broadcasters were from parts of the country where *r*-dropping is essential to the local accent—Mike Wallace from Massachusetts, David Brinkley from North Carolina, Dan Rather from Texas—but they all adopted the rhotic pronunciation recommended by Kenyon. When newsman Bob Schieffer interviewed at CBS, he told his prospective boss he had worked for a TV station in Texas. "We have no interest in anybody with a regional accent," the man said. By "regional," he meant Southern. Schieffer got the job and lost his accent.

It's important to note here that when we talk about regional accents in the Midwest, we're talking about the speech of the white populace. Blacks did not settle in Midwestern cities in large numbers until World War I, when they were recruited to address the sudden shortage of workers in the munitions industries. Once they arrived, they were isolated geographically by restrictive covenants, socially by taboos against intermarriage, and economically by relegation to the dirtiest, lowest-paying jobs, preventing social or professional interaction with whites. As a result, blacks maintained the speech patterns they brought with them from the South, while developing their own distinctive vernacular. When I asked a rapper named

C-Sharp about stereotypically St. Louis pronunciations such as "farty" ("forty") and "worsh" ("wash"), he responded, "That's the white folks. We understand what they're saying, but we don't talk that way ourselves. Like, we'll say 'y'all.'"

Since four of the five most segregated cities in the U.S. are in the Midwest, the region—in particular the heavily industrialized Inland North zone—has a wider divergence between white and black speech than anywhere in the country. However, while African American English was once consistent throughout the country, later generations have adopted some local pronunciations to form distinct "blaccents." For example, the Chicago rapper Common mixes the Southern tendency to drop the *r* in "liar" and "award" with the strongly fronted Inland North *o* in his stage name and "Oscar."

Regional accents aren't just more prevalent among whites, they're more prevalent among certain classes of whites. Television and radio may have standardized accents among broadcasters, but they were not responsible for doing the same to listeners. Radio began broadcasting Kenyon's standardized English into American homes in the 1920s, with no effect on listeners' accents. Nobody watched more TV than the baby boomers, and their accents are more distinctive than the generations who followed them. Regional accents haven't disappeared, they've just become less widespread. What really caused dialect leveling was education and geographic mobility, which were both accelerated by World War II. Young men assigned to platoons with soldiers from all over the country were exposed to people who didn't talk like the folks back home, and had to moderate their accents to make themselves more easily understood. After the war, they went to college on the GI Bill, where English instructors discouraged them from using nonstandard regionalisms such as "clumb" for "climbed," "youse" as a second person plural, and "that needs worshed" for "that needs washing." Today, accents are strongest among whites who have never left their hometowns or graduated from college, and who hold jobs that require little contact with people outside the region: police officers, firefighters, tradespeople, retail clerks, truck drivers, assembly-line workers, hairstylists. (The TV show *Cops* is great for accents.)

I have a friend who grew up in the Upper Peninsula of Michigan, then left to attend Michigan State University, work in the New York publishing industry, and write video games in Los Angeles. When I asked him to describe the meaning and uses of "eh," a common interjection in Michigan, Wisconsin, and Minnesota ("Pretty cold today, eh?"), he responded, "I scrubbed that word from my speech a long time ago." I also know Cincinnatians who have trained themselves not say "please?" when they can't understand an out-of-town business caller. To most of us, "please" is an entreaty, but in Cincinnati, it means "pardon me?"

Despite the Midwest's diversity of dialects, there are some general rules for speaking Midwestern. Some have to do with pronunciation, others with social norms.

• **Talk through your nose.** Midwestern speech, particularly the Inland North and North Central accents, emanates from the top half of the head. Words originate in the upper palate and are directed out the frontal sinus, resulting in a semicongested vibrato. Hoke Colburn, the Georgia chauffeur in *Driving Miss Daisy*, described a woman from Ohio who "talks funny…like her nose is stuffed up." Try talking as though your lower jaw has fallen off and you have to form words with the rest of your face, and you'll be on your way to achieving Midwestern nasality.

• **Don't just pronounce your *r*'s, draw them out as much as possible**. English-language dialects are divided into the rhotic and the non-rhotic. Non-rhotic speakers drop their *r*'s after vowels and at the ends of words. The Bostonian who asks "wheah's the pahty?" is non-rhotic. So are New Yorkers, and many Southerners. Rhotic speakers pronounce *r*'s wherever they appear in a word. Midwestern speech is rhotic in the extreme. Midwesterners don't just pronounce all our *r*'s, we allow them to run on so long they jostle surrounding letters. "Thurrr's a reason yerrr carrr's A/C don't worrrk. You need to refill 'errr with coolant." Don't roll your *r*'s. Growl them. Together, nasality and rhoticity explain why Midwesterners have been said to sound like pirates with head colds.

• **Omit vowels.** While Northeastern and Southern accents turn consonants into vowels, Midwestern accents often omit vowels altogether. This feature can make Midwestern sound hard, or barbed. Take this example, heard in Cedar Rapids, Iowa: "Werr goin' to t' see the drector of the Creer Center on Fridey." Or: "We went to a rest'runt on Saturdey an' had a great steak n' ptayta." Also, you work on your car's injun in a groj.

• **If you must criticize, do so passive-aggressively.** It's been said that in New York, every insult is a compliment: "This is my buddy Jerry. He's been bustin' my balls for thirty years now. Right, Jer?" In the South, on the other hand, every compliment is an insult: "Well, aren't you kind?" In the Midwest, you're never certain whether you're being complimented or insulted. Midwesterners don't like to sound critical or hurt anyone's feelings, so we've developed code words that allow us to avoid stating an opinion altogether. The most important words to know are "interesting" and "different." If something has merit, but you don't personally care for it, it's "interesting."

"What do you think of the Vikings' new stadium?"

"It's interesting."

(The story is told of a consultant who presented an idea to a group of Minnesotans, and thought it was going over well because they all said it was interesting.)

"What do you think of that mural under the Wilson Avenue viaduct of three dolphins copulating with the Queen of the Nile?"

"It's pretty different."

Calling something "different" suggests it violates a social norm, and that therefore, the person who is trying to avoid being insulting has been insulted himself, and would be justified in saying something much stronger—if he were the type of person who violates social norms.

- **Mispronounce foreign names.** Pity the French. LaSalle, Marquette, Jolliet, Cadillac, Hennepin, and Nicolet were the first Europeans to discover and settle the Midwest. They left their names, and the names of their patrons, all over the region—only to have them butchered by subsequent waves of bloody-minded English speakers. Let's start with the Midwest's oldest cities, Detroit and St. Louis. Because of its location at the chokepoint of the Great Lakes, Detroit was originally "d'Etroit," which means "the narrows." The French pronunciation, "Day-TWA," is now only used ironically, by Detroiters trying to make their city sound fancier than it currently is or has ever been. And then there are Detroit's street names. Gratiot is, horrifyingly, "GRASH-it," while Cadieux is "Cad-JOO" and Jos. Campau is "Joseph Compo." St. Louis, of course, was originally pronounced "San LOO-ee," after the 13th-century king-saint. There, Gravois Street is "GRAV-oy," Carondelet has a *t* at the end, and Laclede acquires a long *e* to become "La-CLEEDE." Smaller towns are even worse: Des Plaines, Illinois, is "Dez Planez" and Versailles, Indiana, is "Ver-SALES." These are the understandable errors of nineteenth-century English speakers who had only the written word to go by. Other languages fare no better. Cairo, the town at the tip of the state, where the Mississippi meets the Ohio, is pronounced "KAY-ro." During the patriotic exultation over the Mexican War, many towns were named for battles that the inhabitants had only read about in newspapers. Thus, in Illinois, San Jose is "San Joze" and Sandoval is "Sand Oval."

• **A carbonated beverage is pop, not soda.** Calling a carbonated beverage "pop" is a marker of Midwesternism. On the East and West coasts, it's "soda," in the South it's "Coke," but in the Midwest, it's the sound a cork makes when it's drawn out a bottleneck. Ben and Perry Feigenson, the Detroit bakers who founded Faygo, took note of this, and named their strawberry-flavored drink Faygo Red Pop. Because of the difficulties of keeping the product fresh, Faygo was only sold in Michigan until the 1950s, but became a regional taste after the company developed a filtration system that purified its water. Maps showing the distribution of the word display a nearly perfect overlay with the region we think of as the Midwest. In fact, the line separating soda drinkers from pop drinkers is said to lie between exits 41 and 42 on the New York State Thruway. To the east, in Syracuse, they say "soda." To the west, in Rochester, it's "pop."

• **Say "you guys."** Unlike most languages, English lacks a standard second-person plural. In Spanish, a group of people is addressed as *ustedes*. In German, *ihr*. English speakers have invented a variety of linguistic kludges to deal with this gap.

In the South, "y'all" is an acceptable second-person plural. The North had better solutions. One is "youse," which originated in Ireland among speakers switching from Gaelic to English. Gaelic has a second-person plural, *sibh*, and the Irish thought their newly acquired language ought to have one, too. So they added an *s* to you to make it plural. Irish immigrants brought "youse" to the United States, and it was once widely used in cities where they settled. (It's still widely used in Ireland.) The word can now be heard mainly among older people in ethnic neighborhoods of New York, Philadelphia, Boston, Buffalo, Cincinnati, Chicago, and St. Louis, as well as in the mining communities of Michigan's Upper Peninsula. In Pittsburgh, the word is "yinz," a contraction of the Scots-Irish "you uns."

But of late "youse" and "yinz" have both lost favor to the even more awkward "you guys." The *Dictionary of American*

Regional English defines "you guys" thusly: "orig. chiefly Northern; now widespread. Used as a second pers plu pron; orig used only in reference to males, but now generally used as a genderless pronoun." As the entry indicated, "you guys" was introduced by Northern speakers, and only for groups of men. Now it's used everywhere, for mixed and even all-female groups. Politicians and athletes apply it to the faceless media horde. President Obama ended press conferences with "Thanks you guys; I appreciate it." One obvious problem with "you guys" is that it's gendered. In any other context, "guy" traditionally refers to a male, but a sorority woman will tell her sisters, "Thanks, you guys; I had an awesome time."

"Youse" and "yinz" are used to refer to small groups. A waitress will ask a couple at a diner, "Are youse ready to order?" Larger groups are addressed as "youse guys," which brings us back to the gender question. Both words are much less common than they were in the twentieth century, and are considered less prestigious and less educated than "you guys." In popular culture, "youse" became associated with cab drivers, bartenders, and other blue-collar white ethnics, who were thought of as reactionary and uneducated. Philadelphia mayor Frank Rizzo, a tough-talking Italian ex-cop, said "youse." But baby boomers didn't want to sound like "Archie Bunker types," so they stopped saying "youse."

"I heard it a lot when I was young," a Buffalonian who grew up in the 1940s and '50s told me.

In the South, "y'all" is considered perfectly acceptable among all classes of people (although Northerners think it sounds hayseed). "Youse" should be treated the same way, and take back some of the linguistic territory it has lost to "you guys."

Now that we've established that Midwesterners do, in fact, speak with accents, we're going to find out more about each of the three regional dialects: Inland North, Midland, and North Central. And then we're going to learn words and phrases distinctive to the Midwest, so you'll know what a Chicagoan means when he tells you he's late for an appointment because he ran into gaper's block, or why you should be embarrassed if a Pittsburgher tells you, "Kennywood's open." By the end of this book, you may not be able to speak Midwestern like a native, but when someone asks, "Jeet?" you'll know how to respond.

INLAND NORTH

The first time I visited Houston, I asked a local, "How far is it to Dallas?"

"To where?" she replied. "To Dale's house?"

Using speech patterns acquired during my childhood in industrial Michigan, I had pronounced the name of Texas's second-largest city as "Dayel-is." That's what linguists call "*a* raising," and it's a signature of the Inland North accent, which is spoken from Rochester, N.Y. on the east to St. Louis and Milwaukee on the west, an area roughly coterminous with the Rust Belt.

The Inland North accent originated in the mid-nineteenth century, and was spread through the lower Great Lakes by Yankee settlers migrating west along the Erie Canal and across Lake Erie. The influence of New England and western New York can be seen all over the Upper Midwest. Place names were transplanted—my own hometown of Lansing, Mich., was named for Lansing, N.Y., in the Finger Lakes region, and Saugatuck, Mich., was named for Saugatuck, Conn. The Midwest's private liberal arts colleges were founded by Eastern clergymen seeking to spread the doctrines of abolitionism, women's equality, and temperance. Ohio's Oberlin College and Michigan's Olivet College were both the creation of John Jay Shipherd, a Presbyterian minister educated in Vermont.

Northwestern University, in Evanston, Ill., was founded by Methodists from western New York's Burned-over District, the forcing ground of many of the era's most fervent religious revivals. Cultural geographers such as David Hackett Fischer and Colin Woodard have lumped New England and the Upper Midwest together in a single region called "Greater New England" or "Yankeedom," sharing the values of social reform and communitarianism.

If the Midwest was settled from New England, then why don't Midwesterners talk like New Englanders? Because the first waves of settlement came from western New England, west of the Connecticut River, an isolated agricultural area that was phonologically distinct from coastal Rhode Island, Massachusetts, and Maine. One of the most significant differences was rhoticity. When the Pilgrims arrived in Plymouth in 1620, they almost certainly pronounced their *r*'s, since this was standard speech in England at the time. Fischer writes of immigrants from East Anglia who spoke a "harsh, high-pitched nasal accent" that became known as the "Yankee twang" when introduced to America. That sounds a lot like a modern Inland North accent. However, in the eighteenth century, *r* dropping became fashionable in London, and spread throughout the country, creating the English accent we know today. Due to the British Empire's cultural and commercial influence, this non-rhotic speech was adopted in Atlantic port cities that traded with England. However, the innovation never reached the hinterlands of New England, so when its sons and daughters began moving west, seeking farmland more fertile than the stony soil of the Green Mountains and the Berkshires, they carried with them the traditional English *r* pronunciation. (A classic example of this migration was Stephen Douglas, who left western Vermont in 1833 to seek his fortune in Illinois, where he was elected to the Senate and bought an estate in Chicago.) The Western Reserve, which became northeastern Ohio, was originally claimed by Connecticut, as it lay directly west of that state. Connecticut formed a land company to sell property to New Englanders, and reserved a tract known as the Firelands for residents whose homes had been burned by the British during the Revolution. To this day, the contours of the Western Reserve match the section of Ohio where Inland North is spoken: a "transition zone" separating Inland North speech from Midland speech runs just south of Akron. To use an example of two well-known Ohio natives, actor Fred Willard, who grew up in Shaker Heights, is an Inland North speaker, while basketball coach Bob Knight, who grew up 57 miles south in Massillon, is a Midland speaker.

In Illinois, Inland North speech is heard only in the far northeastern corner of the state, which was settled by New Englanders who followed the Great Lakes to their terminus in Chicago. It's also the dominant accent in the Lower Peninsula of Michigan, and in southeastern Wisconsin, around Milwaukee.

The Inland North accent as we know it today began to develop in the early twentieth century, as a result of one of the most remarkable linguistic transitions of the modern era: the Northern Cities Vowel Shift. Vowels whose pronunciations had been stable for a thousand years, since the days of feudal England, began taking on new inflections in the mouths of Upper Midwesterners. The changes were first detected by linguists doing field research in Chicago and Detroit in the late 1960s. In his book *Dialect Diversity in America*, William Labov describes the Shift as a series, or chain, of pronunciation changes. The Shift affects five different vowel sounds, but Labov believes it was triggered by the short *a* that makes "Dallas" incomprehensible to Texans.

"The logic that connects these five changes resembled a game of 'musical chairs,' in which each inhabitant of a position moves one unit to dislodge the next," Labov wrote. "The initiating event appears to be the shift of short-a in *bat* to a front, raised position, a sound very much like the vowel of *yeah*…Into the gap created by this shift, the vowel of *got* moves forward. In the most extreme form, *cot* sounds like *cat*, *block* like *black*, *socks* like *sacks*…The vowel of *bought* then moves down and front toward this position, along with other members of the 'long open-o' word class: law, talk, cross, dawn, dog, etc… Short-e then shifts to the back toward short-u, producing a confusion between *desk* and *dusk* as short-e enters short-u territory. Most recently, short-u has responded to the intrusion by moving back, producing the potential confusion between *busses* and *bosses*, *cud* and *cawed*…The chain shift has come full circle."

These pronunciations should sound familiar to anyone who has eavesdropped on a conversation between two on-break sales associates at the Golf Mill Mall in Niles, Ill., or ordered a Texas Red Hot from a waitress at Louie's in Buffalo.

"Just in terms of numbers, you're talking about a lot of vowels moving around, that's a pretty significant thing," says linguist Matthew Gordon, now an associate professor of English at the University of Missouri. "Some of these particular vowels, the short *i*, the short *a*, the short *e* those have been pretty stable throughout the history of English, for over a thousand years."

While researching his doctoral thesis, *Small Town Values, Big-City Vowels: A Study of the Northern Cities Shift in Michigan*, Gordon listened to recordings of Grand Rapidians born in the late nineteenth century. None of them produced the vowel inflections associated with the Shift. (Neither did President Gerald Ford, who was raised in Grand Rapids in the 1910s and 20s.)

"When you listen to them, they don't sound at all like modern Michiganders," Gordon says. "All the evidence seems to show the Northern Cities Shift got started some time in the twentieth century, and really got ramped up. Definitely, the first half of the twentieth century was when it progressed to the point you would really hear it like you do today."

But why did the Shift start then, and why has it been confined to the Inland North accent region? Labov theorizes that its origins date back nearly two hundred years, when New Englanders,

New Yorkers, and immigrants arrived in upstate New York to dig the Erie Canal. All had different ways of pronouncing the vowel *a*. Southwestern New Englanders usually raised it, making "Ann" sound like "Ian." Rhode Islanders and Mainers only raised short *a* before nasal consonants—*m* and *n*. Bostonians never did, pronouncing "laugh" and "half" with the *a* in "father." New Yorkers randomly distributed raised and lax *a*'s throughout their vocabulary. From this melting pot of dialects emerged a single system, in which the short *a* was *always* raised. The new dialect then spread westward, as settlers followed the canal into the Great Lakes. Because Yankees were community-minded, with entire towns moving *en masse* to form orderly new Midwestern villages, the Inland North accent is remarkably consistent from one end of the Great Lakes to the other. That's why Chicagoans sound more like Buffalonians than they do like residents of central Illinois.

Charles Boberg of Canada's McGill University believes the Shift was already beginning before the first Midwesterners left Connecticut and Vermont. He cites a late-twentieth-century interview with a man from New Britain, Conn., whose "vowel system approximates those of paradigmatic Northern Cities speakers of the Great Lakes region." Boberg theorizes that Western New England supplied "the pivot conditions for the shift," which then advanced simultaneously there and in the Great Lakes. He concludes that "the origins of the Northern Cities Shift clearly lie on the banks of the lower Connecticut River."

As I pointed out in the introduction, Inland North was once considered "standard" American speech, so much so that the Southern linguist Raven McDavid dubbed it SWINE: Standard White Inland North English. This is no longer the case, due both to changes in the accent, and to its home region's loss of economic and political power. The Northern Cities Vowel Shift, which was less advanced in the 1920s than in later generations, has made Buffalonians, Clevelanders, Detroiters, and Chicagoans sound more distinct from the rest of the country, so much so that *Saturday Night Live* parodied it in two sketches.

"Bill Swerski's Superfans" made "Da Bears" a national catchphrase, and exaggerated the fronted *o*'s of Chicagoans: one of the characters was a south-side Irishman who pronounced his name "Tahhd O'Cahhnor." Another sketch, "1-600-LANSING," was a parody advertisement for a phone sex line for men turned on by women with nasal Michigan accents. The animated sitcom *Family Guy* also once did a cutaway bit about a Wisconsin nymphomaniac who cries "oh Gahhhd" and "oh cray-ep" during sex.

Perhaps as a result, some younger urban Midwesterners have been altering their speech to sound less regional, says David Durian, a native of Chicago's suburbs and an adjunct professor of English at the College of DuPage in Glen Ellyn, Ill. In Chicago, for example, the tendency to replace *th* with *d* or *t* (known as "stops") has been diminishing. It was a product of the fact that most European languages do not contain the *th* sound, known as the interdental fricative. Not even the Irish mastered it when they switched from Gaelic to English, and so "dese, dem, and dose" or "t'ree," "t'rough," and "t'anks" became common pronunciations in immigrant communities. In fact, "Dese, Dem, and Dose Guys" is a term for a certain type of down-to-earth Chicagoan, usually from a white south side neighborhood or an inner-ring suburb. But it's becoming less frequently heard among speakers born after 1970. The sixtysomething auto dealer who sold me a Ford Escape at Bredemann Ford in Glenview, Ill., did it, but his twentysomething assistant didn't. The same is not true in some blue-collar neighborhoods and suburbs, though. Durian reports some younger speakers in suburbs like Brookfield or Riverside, and city neighborhoods like Bridgeport, continue to use it. I used to go to the racetrack with a guy from the inner-ring suburb of Burbank. Whenever I cashed a bet, he'd exclaim, "Dayt's awesome!" Blame its demise in middle class speech on the Superfans.

"It's become so stereotyped as a pronunciation, and it's pointed out so often in speech that some people are actually shifting away from it," Durian says.

This feature of the Chicago accent was most widespread during the city's industrial heyday. Blue-collar work and strong regional speech are closely connected: if you graduated from high school in the 1960s, you didn't need to go to college, or even leave your neighborhood, to get a good job, and once you got that job, you didn't have to talk to anyone outside your house, your factory, your tavern, or your parish. A regular Joe accent was a sign of masculinity and local cred, bonding forces important for the teamwork of industrial labor. A 1970s study of steelworker families on Chicago's East Side by linguist Robin Herndobler found that women were less likely than their husbands to say "dese, dem, and dose," because they dealt with doctors, teachers, and other professionals. After the mills closed, kids went to college, where they learned not to say "dat," and took office jobs requiring interaction with people outside the neighborhood.

(Something similar is happening in Buffalo, which, like Chicago, had large-scale immigration from Ireland and Poland, and a steel industry that shut down during the deindustrialization of the 1980s. I know a Buffalonian from the baby boom generation who doesn't fully pronounce *th*, but every Gen Xer and Millennial I've met there does.)

In fact, Durian is beginning to hear the Northern Cities Vowel Shift weaken among young, middle class speakers in the Chicago area born after the late 1970s. Durian and his colleague, University of Illinois-Chicago linguist Richard Cameron, have been working on a project called *Five Generations of Language Change in Chicago,* in which they are looking at changes to the Chicago accent since the late 1800s. To do so, they have been analyzing speech differences among speakers born as early as 1875, by comparing recordings they themselves made in recent years with recordings made by the linguist Lee Pederson during a dialect study he conducted in 1962-1963. Durian and Cameron have been finding that the short *o* "box" vowel is backing up among some young middle class speakers, bringing it closer to the "cot-caught" merger, while the short *a*, after being raised a little bit higher by each generation of Chicagoans since the early 1900s, seems to have plateaued among young middle class speakers, advancing as high as it can go. However, young working class Chicagoans still use the same fronted *o*'s and raised *a*'s as their parents and grandparents, the baby boomers and World War II veterans who spoke the classic Chicago accent caricatured by "Superfans" creator George Wendt, who grew up in a white ethnic neighborhood on Chicago's southwest side.

To those interested in the connection between accents and cultural identity, there is something poignant about the "Superfans" sketches. They captured that accent, and the people who spoke it, at a time when both were ceasing to define what it meant to be a Chicagoan. In the mid-1980s, when the Superfans' beloved coach Mike Ditka led "da Bears" to the Super Bowl, the city's steel mills were closing, threatening the livelihoods of Chicago's working class. After a half century of Irish mayors, city hall was under the control of an African-American, Harold Washington, who was almost unanimously opposed by white ethnics, the community most associated with the classic Chicago accent. Chicagoese, as newspaper columnist Mike Royko called the dialect, was the language of hardworking, traditional, churchgoing, neighborhood-loyal people who had advanced from immigrant to middle class in two generations. Ditka, himself a Slav from a Pennsylvania steel town, understood (and was part of) the team's appeal to his fellow ethnics. He dubbed his players "Grabowskis," suggesting that, like a Polish plumber or steelworker, they were tough pluggers who got the job done. The classic Chicago accent is heard less often these days because the white working class is less numerous, and less influential, than it was in the twentieth century. It has been pushed to the margins of city life, both figuratively and geographically, by multiculturalism and globalization: the accent is most prevalent in blue-collar suburbs and in all-white neighborhoods in the northwest and southwest corners of the city, which are heavily populated by city workers whose families have lived in Chicago for generations. Beginning in the 1990s, Chicago became a regional business and financial capital, attracting college graduates from Ohio and Indiana who speak a more neutral strain of Midwestern. It has also attracted Third World immigrants who are not adopting the "classic" accent. As what it means to be a Chicagoan changes, so does what a Chicagoan sounds like.

Inland North's rise to linguistic distinction and its subsequent subsumation into generic American speech among younger middle class speakers may turn out to be coeval with the industrial Midwest's own rise and decline. "When [Midwestern cities] were going through a period of growth, up until about 1950, the times that the Northern Cities Shift was most active were up through that sort of World War II period," Durian says. "And then what happens from 1950 to 2000, you see the Northern Cities Shift slowly beginning to shift towards eroding. So it seemed that as the population decreased in these cities, that's also had an impact on the shift beginning to erode. Possibly among some younger speakers, we may be starting to see the emergence of a more generic American accent. ... I think regional identity still matters to some extent to these kinds of speakers, but I don't think it matters as much as it did fifty years ago. I think now some people are more likely to identify with the idea that you're a Midwesterner, rather than a Chicagoan or a Buffalonian. That may be having some influence on reducing some of those stronger characteristics."

As the Upper Midwest has become less powerful, less populous and less influential, so has its native accent. Now, some linguists argue, the Midland accent—heard in Columbus, Cincinnati, Indianapolis and Peoria—has replaced Inland North as the most "neutral" American dialect.

"One may hypothesize that the Inland North dialect is in decline in reaction to the failure of the industrial economy in the rust belt," wrote Thomas S. Donahue. "The ruralized speech of the North Midland area has encroached as the old social and economic promises implied in the mastery of SWINE have folded and all but disappeared."

There may be cultural and political reasons for this as well. On political matters, the Inland North dialect region is still closely allied with New England, its cultural hearth. William Labov found that counties where Inland North is spoken support Democratic presidential candidates more strongly than Midland-speaking counties. As the country has become polarized along party and regional lines, southerners may find the voices of Midlanders more relatable than those of urban northerners, who hail from a place they find politically antagonistic. Northerners certainly read fewer cultural assumptions into a Midland accent than a Southern accent. The so-called Midlands have become the great swing region of American politics, and the great swing region of American accents, as well.

KEY FEATURES OF THE INLAND NORTH DIALECT

- Raised a, which makes "cat" sound like "cayet."

- Fronted o, which makes "box" sound like "bahhx."

- Lack of the "low-back merger," in which "cot" and "caught" are pronounced identically. Only in the Great Lakes and the mid-Atlantic do they sound different. (Think of a New Yorker saying "cawfee.") In Minnesota, both words sound like "cahht." In Cincinnati, they sound more like "cawt."

- "Canadian raising" of the i vowel. Inland North speakers raise this vowel in most situations, producing a sharp, high-pitched sound in words such as "fire" or "guys."

MIDLAND

On May 1, 1969, Fred Rogers, beloved host of *Mister Rogers' Neighborhood*, charmed a crusty Rhode Island senator into appropriating $20 million for educational television.

"My first program was on WQED fifteen years ago, and its budget was thirty dollars," Rogers told Sen. John O. Pastore. He pronounced the word program as "progrum." Ago sounded like "ag-ao." And the *o* in dollar was backed, so the word came out as "dawler."

A native of Latrobe, Penn., who produced his program in Pittsburgh, Rogers was probably the best-known speaker of the Midland dialect. He was undoubtedly the most widely heard, since *Mister Rogers' Neighborhood* aired every weekday on public television stations from 1966 until 2006.

Most viewers probably didn't think of Rogers as having an accent, certainly not in the same way as contemporaneous TV figures Andy Griffith and Archie Bunker. But he did. While it wasn't the heavy Yinzer accent of a Pittsburgh steelworker, it recognizably belonged to the dialect region of western Pennsylvania and eastern Ohio. Ohio Gov. John Kasich, who grew up in McKees Rocks, Penn., has the same accent. In ads for his 2016 presidential campaign, he talked about how his "fawther, Big Jawn," was a mail carrier. Yet unlike New Yorker Bernie Sanders or southerner Jimmy Carter, Kasich's speech has never been parodied, or even commented upon.

That's because the Midland accent, as its name suggests, is the most middle American and least othered of the Midwestern dialects. It occupies the space between the Inland North and Appalachian accents—a latitudinal band from western Pennsylvania to eastern Iowa—and serves as a transition zone between them, just as that same region serves to mediate the political and cultural extremes of the North and the South. Ohio is the swing state of American politics, having voted for the winning presidential candidate in 13 consecutive elections. Rascal Flatts, a band from Columbus, is not quite country and not quite rock and roll. And the Midland accent does not really register with northern or southern ears.

"If you place a Midland accent for a lot of people, it's speech that a lot of people think is accent free," says Kathryn Campbell-Kibler, an Ohio State University professor who studies social reactions to speech. "Not very many people think the Midland accent is an accent in that social sense. Only a small subset of northern Ohio thinks central Ohio has an accent."

Midland speech occupies "a transitional area from the Northern edge to the South," says Erik Thomas, a central Ohio native who now teaches linguistics at North Carolina State University. "People in most parts of the country wouldn't notice it was very different. Generally speaking, in some ways, it's a national average, because it's the middle of the country. Pronunciations are on a gradient, and it's in the middle of the gradient."

Nonetheless, the Midland accent has its own history, lexicon and phonology. It even has a sub-dialect—Pittsburghese—that's one of the most colorful American languages.

The Midland accent has its roots in the port cities of the mid-Atlantic, particularly Philadelphia, which was a debarkation point for Scots-Irish immigrants who began fleeing Ulster's religious conflicts in the early eighteenth century. By the time they arrived, most of the coastal land had been claimed, so they moved inland, following Daniel Boone's Wilderness Road through the Cumberland Gap to the Ohio River, and later, the National Road from Cumberland, Md., to Vandalia, Ill. That macadam turnpike was completed in the 1830s, the same decade the Black Hawk War cleared the Midwest for settlement; from then on, New England Yankees and Scots-Irish from Pennsylvania, Maryland and Virginia followed parallel paths westward, bringing their linguistic proclivities with them. (Abraham Lincoln had a typical Midlander background. His family moved from Virginia to Kentucky to Indiana, before settling on a farm in east-central Illinois. No recordings of Lincoln exist, but in his Oscar-winning performance, Daniel Day-Lewis delivered an accent that put me in mind of a modern politician from central Illinois, former Gov. Jim Edgar. Day-Lewis did his research in the National Archives, where he listened to recordings of people who grew up in the regions of Kentucky and Indiana where Lincoln was raised.) To this day, traces of Ulster speech can be heard in the Lower Midwest. The construction of needs without "to be," as in "that needs washed," goes back to Ireland. So does the word "run" for a small stream. Turkey Run, a state park in central Indiana, is an example. The plus comparative—"that's all the further I could run"—also originated in Ireland.

Midland speech is less uniform than Inland North, because the Scots-Irish organized themselves by clan, while the Yankees organized themselves into communities based on religion and ideology.

"Yankees moved in whole towns, and built permanent settlements with houses by the roadside," wrote William Labov. "This created the environment in which generation after generation of child language learners transmitted the system intact. On the other hand, Upland Southerners moved in isolated clusters, and often relocated with houses scattered along creeks and springs. As a consequence, Midland cities show a wide variety of dialect formation: Philadelphia, Pittsburgh, Columbus, Cincinnati, Indianapolis and St. Louis are all quite different."

There are, though, some common characteristics of Midland speech:

• **Intrusive r:** Saying "worsh" for "wash" or calling the nation's capital "Worshington" is heard from Pittsburgh to St. Louis. However, like many regional idiosyncracies, it has become less common as outsiders comment on it. Former Indiana University basketball coach Bob Knight, born in 1940, told an audience of Donald Trump supporters that if they voted for the candidate, "they're gonna put you right next to our Founding Fathers and George Worshington." But it's rarer among speakers born after World War II.

Why did *r* intrude on "wash"? One theory is that before the "cot-caught" merger spread to the Midlands, "ah" sounded like *o*. Older Philadelphians, for example, still say "wooter" for "water." The similarity to the *o* in "or" may have made it seem logical to insert that letter.

• **Positive anymore:** Among most English speakers, "anymore" denotes something that's no longer happening, as in, "Oh, that store's not open anymore." In the Midlands, however, it can be used to indicate continuing action.

"Anymore, there's so much traffic you can hardly drive there."
Or:
"Anymore, it's too dangerous to go downtown."

Here, "anymore" is similar in meaning to "nowadays." I first heard the positive anymore when I worked as a newspaper reporter in Decatur, Ill., a Midland-speaking city midway between Indianapolis and St. Louis. Like many other Midland features, the usage originated in Northern Ireland, and can still be heard there.

• **Fronted *o*:** Among heavily accented Midland speakers, the word "no" sounds like "nao," and "ozone" like "aozaone." This pronunciation is shared with their distant cousins in Philadelphia and Baltimore, the cities from which the Midland accent derives.

• **The "cot-caught" merger:** This pronunciation feature is rapidly becoming standard English. Given the Midlands' role as a linguistic bellwether, it's no surprise that it has recently spread into the region. It's an example of Midland's divergence from Inland North, which has so far proven impregnable to the merger, and also of generational change, since speakers who say "worsh" don't pronounce "cot" and "caught" the same way.

• **All the plus comparative:** "Is that all the better they can do?" or "Is that all the bigger they can get?" are classic Midland locutions.

PITTSBURGHESE

No Midwestern city is more conscious than Pittsburgh of the way it speaks—or, more accurately, the way it used to speak. In the Strip District, Pittsburgh-themed gift shops sell placards and puzzles with lists of words and pronunciations that define the dialect locals proudly call Pittsburghese: jagoff, hoagie, telepole, jumbo, nebby, slippy. "Dahntahn" for "downtown." "Spicket" for spigot. "Stillers" for Steelers. Above their Keystone State license plates, Pittsburghers paste stickers with the phrase "n 'at," a shortening of "and that" which is tacked on to the ends of sentences to mean, roughly, "et cetera."

Pittsburghese developed among immigrant steelworkers from Poland, Bohemia, Hungary, and Croatia. Derisively called "Polacks" and "Hunkies" by "old stock" Americans, they sought a language and identity that would provide solidarity against nativist prejudice. This was reinforced by the labor struggles of the 1930s and '40s, which inspired previously competitive ethnic groups to band together for economic advancement. In his essay "On the eastern edge of the Heartland: Two industrial city dialects," Thomas S. Donahue calls Pittsburghese a "koine," a dialect formed in a melting pot of languages. To traditional Scots-Irish phrases such as "jag" for thorn and "redd up" for clean were added the Eastern European "babushka" and "pierogi."

"In mill towns like Pittsburgh," wrote Donahue, "where steel production dominated the economy through the Second World War, the dialect was shared and reinforced in five domains: at work, in family life at home, and in social outings at places like family bars, at school and in contexts related to worship at Roman Catholic churches. Oral history evidence shows that the dialect was reinforced and spread by socially interactive people who worked in retail sales [in shops, grocery stores, butchers, clothiers, gasoline stations and garages] by persons who catered to a working class clientele. It is crucial to understand that the dialect began in a sexually segregated male workplace, that it developed an initial cohesion among the dominant Roman Catholic religion of its speakers, and that in the middle of the twentieth century was spoken by a large but distinctive group who had a common unionized mission of working toward an additional advantage in the workplace."

These were all elements of a provincial, insular culture, and they were reinforced even more by geography. Situated on the western slope of the Allegheny Mountains, Pittsburgh had developed a dialect distinct from the rest of Pennsylvania even before the steel mills arrived. And its neighborhoods were separated by hills and rivers, which discouraged social mixing.

The prototypical Pittsburgh word is "yinz." The equivalent of "youse," it's a contraction of the Scots-Irish "you uns." It's so uniquely Pittsburgh that "Yinzer" is a term for a heavily-accented local who dresses in black and gold to show his love for the Steelers, the Pens, and the Buccos, and drinks a lot of "Arn City" beer.

The archetypal Yinzer was Myron Cope. Born to a Jewish family in 1929, he became an acclaimed journalist for *Sports Illustrated* and the *Saturday Evening Post*. Despite his professional advancement, Cope never lost his Pittsburgh accent. That was one reason the Steelers hired him in 1970 as a color commenter for their radio broadcasts. He held that job for 35 years and five Super Bowl victories, becoming in the process the voice of Pittsburghese. His commentary was nearly unintelligible to anyone outside western Pennsylvania, but his *Yiddishkeit* cries of "yoi!", "double yoi!" and "triple yoi!" at thrilling plays became Pittsburgh catchphrases.

"Oh, I'm tellin' ya, that school's aht," Cope exulted when running back Jerome "The Bus" Bettis fought off three Seattle Seahawks defenders. "Da schoolbell rang. Da kiddies, dey all jumped ahn Da Bus and dere went Da Bus steamin' aht of the schoolyard or sumpin' and three Seattle Seahawks trahd to get on Da Bus and dey wouldn't open the doors. Fahnly one of 'em bring him dahn."

Cope conceived "The Terrible Towel," a gold-colored rally cloth for Steelers fans to twirl over their heads. From his mouth, however, it came out as "The Terrible Tahhl." Monophthongization—that is, turning a double-stepped vowel into a single sound—is a hallmark of Pittsburgh pronunciation. At work on "ow," it transforms "downtown" to "dahntahn" and "house" to "hahs." With long *i*, monophthongization makes "fire" sound like "fahr" and "Pirates" like "Pahrtz." I heard the story of a Pittsburgh actor who was asked to say "tire iron" in a play. He found the line so difficult the director changed it to "crowbar."

Pittsburgh has changed dramatically since the 1980s. The Homestead Works, once the world's largest steel mill, shut down in 1986, and was eventually replaced with a shopping mall—and the steel crisis changed the Pittsburgh accent. Men laid off by the mills were forced to move to the Sun Belt to find jobs. In their new hometowns, they realized they had funny accents, and toned them down to fit in with the neighbors. Instead of graduating from high school straight to the mills, the children of those who stayed behind went to college, where they met classmates from outside Pittsburgh, and were discouraged from using Pittsburghisms such as "yinz" and "n' at." The city became a destination for doctors, academics, and artists, not all of them Pittsburgh natives. As a result of these economic and demographic changes, Pittsburghese has been transformed from everyday speech to a legacy dialect used self-consciously to express local pride.

"Terms such as 'Yinz,' 'Jagoff' and 'Dahntahn' were adopted as emblems of authentic Pittsburghness, even as younger generations stopped using them in everyday speech, to avoid sounding blue collar and provincial," wrote Carnegie Mellon University professor Barbara Johnstone in her book *Speaking Pittsburghese: The Story of a Dialect*. For young, middle-class Pittsburghers, "certain stereotypical pronunciations, words, and structures are available for performance and allusions to localness that mock the stereotyped working-class Pittsburgher of the industrial era, and in doing so, project and are heard by their peers as projecting local knowledge and post-industrial hipness."

I met a young man at sports memorabilia shop called, of course, Yinzers, who said a high school teacher had instructed him to say "you guys" instead of "yinz." He was proud of his accent, and perplexed that even Pittsburghers thought it was incorrect.

"I think it's what makes us unique as a city," he said.

Actor Curt Wootton grew up in a suburb of Pittsburgh, but he's not a genuine Yinzer. He plays one on YouTube, though. Wootton is the star of "Pittsburgh Dad," a popular series of short videos featuring a character expressing his exasperation with the modern world in an exaggerated Pittsburgh accent: "Nah, nah, nah, we ain't controlling the whole hahs with a cell phone. Deb, you lose your cell phone all the time. Then some yahoo who fahnd it dahn T.J. Maxx has control of our thermostat? Ah-ah-ah. Ah-ah-ah."

"The original inspiration was definitely Curt's own father, but everyone would be dying because he sounded like *everyone's* dad," said co-creator Chris Preksta, who graduated from Steel Valley High School in Munhall, Pa.

As in Chicago, as Pittsburgh becomes less industrialized and more professionalized, it is developing a dialect less distinct from the rest of the country, especially among middle-class speakers. Yet it still celebrates the speech of the World War II and baby boom generations as the "classic" or "authentic" Pittsburgh accent. In the words of a young woman grilling sandwiches at Primanti Bros., as Pittsburgh an institution as there is, "We don't say yinz; our parents say yinz."

Virginia Montanez, a popular local blogger known as PittGirl, had her own reaction to "Pittsburgh Dad." After noting that her father talked just like Wootton's character, telling his children to worsh their feet, she argued that it's time to redefine "the quintessential Pittsburgher."

"We're trying to pull 'quintessential Pittsburgher' out of the box that says he's a blue-collar worker with an unmelodic accent who lives and breathes Steelers football while working to support his wife and four children with a job in the mill," she wrote. "He eats various forms of fat for breakfast and leftover city chicken for lunch and spends his evenings stomping through the house turning off lights that are brightening empty rooms. His hands never are fully clean. He uses the basement potty. All of his clothes come from Hills."

Meanwhile, Montanez continued, "We're trying to shove the quintessential Pittsburgher into the box that says he or she is a white-collar, college-educated, stylish cosmopolitan who dresses in brand names, frequents upscale 'foodie-friendly' restaurants, orders flat whites from Starbucks and would rather go hungry than be seen buying even a pack of gum at Walmart.

"Here's the next truth-bomb: Both of those versions of Pittsburgher exist. In fact, there are Pittsburghers on every spot of the spectrum from one box to the next."

And just as there's now more than one way of being a Pittsburgher, there's more than one way of talking like a Pittsburgher.

ST. LOUIS: THE LINGUISTIC ISLAND

Given where it lies on the map, St. Louis should be a Midland-speaking city. After Pittsburgh, Columbus, and Indianapolis, it's the next major city on Interstate 70, and it's directly west of Cincinnati. However, because it was a major industrial city, and because it sits on a highway that connects it with Chicago, St. Louis has been seceding from the Midland dialect region, and joining the Inland North.

The most stereotypical St. Louis pronunciation is "farty" for "forty." St. Louisans swap an "ar" for an "or" sound, so they eat "carn on the cob" and wish each other "good marning." This is unique to St. Louis, but the city has other features in common with the Midlands. Older St. Louisans say "worsh" for "wash," "wants off" for "wants to get off," and "I waited on him" instead of "I waited for him."

Founded by the French in 1764 as a sanctuary after the loss of the French and Indian War, St. Louis is older than any other Midland city but Pittsburgh. At the confluence of the Missouri and Mississippi rivers, it was a hub of the nineteenth-century river trade. In 1904, the year it hosted the World's Fair and the Olympics, St. Louis was the nation's fourth-largest city, behind New York, Philadelphia, and Chicago. It was a center of brewing, milling, and meat packing, and a magnet for Irish and Italian immigrants. That gave St. Louis, and its dialect, a more urban character than most other Midland cities. For example, older St. Louisans still say "youse" and substitute *d* for *th*.

It was a highway, though, that cemented St. Louis's linguistic allegiance. In 1926, Route 66 was completed, linking St. Louis and Chicago. The National Road, a major migration route for Midlanders, hadn't quite made it to St. Louis, stopping at Vandalia, Ill. Route 66 became an avenue for the southwesterly spread of the Northern Cities Vowel Shift, planting it in the mouths of speakers in Bloomington, Springfield, and St. Louis. When Interstate 55 bypassed the Illinois cities, Northern speech receded there. But St. Louis, a destination city, became more firmly allied with Inland North. According to the *Atlas of North American English*, "St. Louis is losing its traditional dialect, with a merger of *are* and *or*, in favor of the Northern Cities Shift of the Chicago area, and the corridor along Route I-55 shows the direction of influence." Lauren A. Friedman calls this a "dialect breach," and observes that the Northern Cities shift did not spread to Central Illinois communities on either side of the highway.

When I lived in Decatur, Ill., 40 miles west of Springfield, people were intensely aware that their speech differed from Chicago's. Chicago dominates its state like few other cities, so Chicago broadcasters and politicians are heard on TV and radio stations throughout Illinois, fostering a sense that downstate is a colony of the big city.

"You talk just like those people up north!" more than one Decaturite told me.

St. Louis, on the other hand, feels more connected to Chicago than it does to the rest of Missouri, which it regards as a hillbilly backwater. A St. Louisan is far more likely to visit Chicago than Kansas City—or Branson, for Pete's sake. The baseball rivalry between the Cubs and the Cardinals unites the cities, rather than dividing them, as fans travel back and forth along I-55 to cheer in enemy territory.

"St. Louis is the only city outside the Great Lakes that participates in the Northern Cities Vowel Shift," says Randy Vines, who studies the St. Louis language as owner of StL Style, a boutique that sells T-shirts with such local sayings as "Highway

Farty" and "Where'd You Go to High School?"

"St. Louis has more in common with the northern and eastern cities than the rest of Missouri," says Vines. "You go 35 miles out, and there's a major difference."

St. Louis's transformation from Midland to Inland North can be heard by listening to two prominent natives born on either side of World War II: Mike Shannon, a Cardinals outfielder and broadcaster born in 1939, and actor John Goodman, born in 1952. Shannon is a Southern-tinged Midland speaker. The Cardinals' National League rivals are the "Worshington Nationals," while a pitcher throws a "ninety-six mahl an ahr fastball." However, Shannon occasionally raises an *a*—the first stirring of the Northern Cities Shift. As exurban Chicago working stiff Dan Conner on the sitcom *Roseanne*, Goodman delivered a completely authentic Inland North accent, calling his wife "Rose-ayen," and his sister-in-law "Jaya-ckie." It wasn't an act. In interviews, he says "hay-end" for "hand" and "shahht" for "shot." Goodman sounds far more like a Chicagoan than does a speaker from Vandalia, Ill., a town 70 miles to the northeast where the Midland accent is beginning to take on southern characteristics.

From a generational and class perspective, neither man's speech is surprising. Shannon is a prewar baby whose father was a police officer. He never graduated from college and has spent his career in the all-male world of baseball. Goodman also came from a working-class background—his widowed mother worked as a waitress and took in laundry—but he attended college and then went to New York to pursue acting. Thomas E. Murray, the leading expert on St. Louis speech, found that modern St. Louisans have consciously rejected speech that sounds "country" or unsophisticated in favor of urban, northern locutions. The "farty" pronunciation has been relegated to the same linguistic ash heap as "dahntahn" and "yinz" have in Pittsburgh, and for the same reason: it sounds "working class." (I didn't spend a lot of time in

St. Louis while researching this book, but the only person I heard say "farty" was a waitress in a diner, who took an order by asking a couple, "What can I get youse?") In his essay "The Language of St. Louis," Murray wrote that "members of the upper class, females, and young informants tend to use Northern and North Midland speech; members of the lower class, males, and elderly informants, however, tend to use Southern and South Midland forms."

In no other Midwestern city have so many dialects intersected, but it's clear which one is winning.

NORTH CENTRAL

At a movie theater in a Minneapolis suburb, a man walked out of an afternoon screening of *Fargo*, and delivered a one-word review more devastating than a Siskel and Ebert thumbs down. "Well," he grumbled, according to the *New York Times*, "that was different."

The state of Minnesota has a complicated relationship with *Fargo* (1996), which was written, produced, and directed by brothers Joel and Ethan Coen, who grew up in a Twin Cities suburb in the 1950s and '60s. On the one hand, it provided a lot of work for local actors and showcased such landmarks as the Paul Bunyan statue in Brainerd, where heroine Marge Gunderson was police chief. On the other hand, it stereotyped Minnesotans as overagreeable yokels who speak a sing-songy English larded with such corny sayings as "you betcha" and "yer darn tootin'." Even today, saying "I didn't like *Fargo*" is a good way to ingratiate yourself with a Minnesotan.

Larissa Kokernot was a Minneapolis stage actor when the Coen brothers cast her as Hooker #1 (the prostitute who reveals that Steve Buscemi's character "wasn't circumcised"). She was also enlisted to work as a dialect coach for Frances McDormand, who won an Academy Award for her role as Marge. Kokernot delivered the most authentic Minnesota accent in the movie, and director

Joel Coen decided he wanted McDormand to sound like her. So the actors spent an afternoon together, during which Kokernot schooled McDormand not only on the technical aspects of Minnesota speech, but the social forces that produced it.

"We talked about nodding: being agreeable and wanting agreement," says Kokernot, who spoke to me about her experience making *Fargo*. "Even if you're making a statement, you're wanting agreement. It's that Norwegian thing of, 'We're not going to get through these winters without working together.' And then the 'ooo' sounds, like in 'knooow.' We talked about the musicality of it, going back to Norwegian. And then how it flattens out a bit. It's very forward. It comes out of the top of the mouth. We talked about the 'yah,' because the 'yah' lives in the same place."

In the service of black comedy, the Coen brothers thought it would be funny to hear characters talking about murder in chirpy, exaggerated Up North accents. The result was so memorable that it put Minnesota on the dialectical map.

"Canadian had a national profile," Kokernot says. "I don't think people had an idea of what Minnesotan sounded like. There was something about that movie, people focused in on that Minnesota sound. I do feel like it has that cachet now. I put in on my resume as one of my dialects: Minnesotan."

So how accurate is the *Fargo* accent? In the winter of 2016, I spent a week in Brainerd. It's a wonderful place to cross-country ski, curl, ice fish, and snowmobile. It is not, however, a place to hear people talk like Marge Gunderson or Jerry Lundegaard, the hapless car salesman whose scheme to have two lowlifes kidnap his wife and hold her for ransom sets the movie's plot in motion. You won't hear it at Yesterday's Gone Bar & Grill. Nor at Ernie's on Gull, the supper club where I enjoyed walleye and a Brandy Alexander. Nor in the fish house where I caught a perch with Bobby Adams, the handyman at Kavanaugh's Resort. Nor at the city council meeting, the Antique Snowmobile Rendezvous, or the Brainerd Lakes Curling Association. There's only one place in Brainerd to hear vowels as drawn out as those of Marge and Jerry. That's in the oral history archives of the Crow Wing County Historical Society, which contains taped interviews conducted in the 1970s with rural Minnesotans born in the early twentieth century; many were children of Norwegian immigrants who spoke the Old World language at home. One interviewer identifies himself as "Bill Hansen of Brainerd, Minnesohhta." When his subject talks about losing her American citizenship by marrying a Norwegian, he responds, "Oh, when ya married him you were a citizen of Norway then, ooh, f'r a little vhile 'til he got his papers straight."

That accent, heavily influenced by Scandinavian inflections, would still have been common among older Minnesotans when the Coen brothers were growing up. But they left for college in New York in the mid-1970s. By the time they returned to film *Fargo*, twenty years later, the accent they set out to caricature was dead and buried, or living in a nursing home. So were some of the phrases that made their way into the script. "Yes sir, you betcha," an enthusiastic affirmative meant to exemplify Minnesotans' agreeableness, is today mostly used in the context of mocking stereotypically Minnesotan behavior. At Jax Café in Minneapolis, I asked the steward if the restaurant served lutefisk, a tasteless, lye-treated piece of whitefish that Minnesotans eat at Christmastime to remember the ocean voyages of their Norwegian ancestors.

"Oh, you betcha," he said, with a smirk.

To my ear, the best Minnesota accent ever committed to film was delivered by Kurt Russell, who played 1980 U.S. Olympic hockey coach Herb Brooks—a Twin Cities-area native—in the movie *Miracle*. Russell's accent is clipped, brisk, nasal, capturing the no-nonsense nature of the man he's portraying, as well as the practicality and restraint of Minnesotans. Both Russell and McDormand realized that the Minnesota accent originates from the front of the mouth, but Russell understood that it emerges from the nose, while McDormand's distended vowels vibrate off her palate—in pursuit of the comic effect the Coen brothers were seeking, she overemphasizes the forwardness of words' origins. McDormand won Best Actress, but Russell gets a gold statue for speaking Minnesotan. McDormand later delivered a more subtle Minnesota accent in *North Country*, a movie about a sexual harassment case in an Iron Range taconite mine. While researching the local dialect, the actors were asked, "You're not going to do that *Fargo* accent, are you?" They didn't.

"I definitely felt like they were trying to hold onto the seriousness of that story, so instead of leaning into it, they were backing," Kokernot observes. "It wasn't that the sounds aren't there; they didn't lean into them as much."

Unlike most Midwesterners, Minnesotans are highly conscious of the way they speak, and of how the rest of the country hears them.

"Whenever I go to an event out of state, people say, 'You're from Minnesota, aren't you?'" Dave Guenther, an art teacher and snowmobile enthusiast from Pequot Lakes, told me when I visited Brainerd.

This self-consciousness predates *Fargo*. It's been a long-running source of humor on the public radio program *A Prairie Home Companion*, founded by Minnesotan Garrison Keillor, and broadcast nationwide from St. Paul. One of the show's writers, Howard Mohr, published a book titled *How to Talk Minnesotan*, which caricatures Minnesotans' reputation for being inoffensive and self-effacing, a trait known as "Minnesota Nice." Sample advice: never accept food from a Minnesotan until you're asked three times.

"Abrupt and eager acceptance of any offer is a common mistake made by Minnesota's visitors. If a Minnesotan says:
Can I get you a cup of coffee?
You should not say:

Yeah, that would be great, thanks, with a little cream and sugar. And how about one of those cookies.

We never accept until the third offer and then reluctantly. On the other hand, if a Minnesotan does not make an offer three times, it's not serious."

Minnesota is in the heart of the North Central dialect region, which also includes the Upper Peninsula of Michigan, northern Wisconsin, northern Iowa, and the eastern Dakotas. Like Inland North and Midland, it is coterminous with a pattern of migration, in this case, of Germans and Scandinavians who arrived in the late nineteenth century, often settling on land too far north to be useful to native-born farmers, and working in extractive industries such as logging and mining. The newcomers transposed elements of their native languages onto English. Norwegian and Swedish both have pitch patterns, in which words' meanings differ according to pronunciation. They also include many words with elongated vowels. Those features contributed to the sing-songy cadence heard among Scandinavian immigrants and their descendants. From Swedish, Minnesotans acquired monophthongization. "Know" is pronounced by slightly dropping the pitch of the *o*. In Minnesota, this results in "knoooow" for know, and "Minnesohhta" for the name of the state.

Like Pittsburghers, Minnesotans' speech consciousness has led them to claim as cultural touchstones words and phrases now only used ironically. Gift shops sell "Uff Da" T-shirts, advertising a Norwegian phrase that means, roughly, "oy vey" or "ay caramba." Young Minnesotans may have heard Grandpa Larsen use it when he was trying to loosen a bolt on the furnace cover, but they don't use it among their friends in Minneapolis, except as a goof.

The German influence on North Central speech is strong in Wisconsin, which was a destination for refugees fleeing the failed revolution of 1848. To this day, German words, pronunciations, and sentence structures are part of the Wisconsin lexicon. The most obvious is "yah," from the German *ja*, for yes. It's both a statement of agreement, and a conversational cue meaning, "I'm listening; go on." It's part of the greeting "Yah hey dere," which is to Wisconsin what "you betcha" is to Minnesota. Budweiser filmed a Wisconsinized version of its "Wassup" commercial, with Cheeseheads shouting "Yah hey dere!" into their cell phones from a tavern, a Packer game, and a deer camp. "Dere," of course, is a legacy of the fact that German, Scandinavian, and other immigrant languages lack the interdental fricative, or "th" sound. Another example is "borrow." In the German settlement areas of Wisconsin, someone might ask, "Can you borrow me five dollars?" In colloquial German, *borgen* can either mean "to borrow" or "to lend." German immigrants assigned the same definitions to its English equivalent.

Some Wisconsinites add "no" or "not" to the end of a sentence as a tag question—an interrogative intended to invite a response from a listener. As in, "It's getting cold today, no?" Or "Brewers gonna have a good season this year, not?" This comes from *nicht*, which performs that function at the end of German sentences. "By" is used like *bei*, which can mean "at" or "to." (*Wilkommen bei McDonald's* is a sign outside fast food restaurants in Berlin.) When a Wisconsinite says, "We had dinner by Steve's," he or she means "We had dinner over at Steve's house." This also resulted in "how's by you?" a now mostly ironic Wisconsinism that roughly translates to, "What's happening in your neck of the woods?"

"Come with" is a common phrase throughout the Midwest: "We're goin' over to Jim's. You wanna come with?" This derives from a German construction in which *mit* functions as a particle, the same way "up" does in "pick it up." In German, *Er kommt mit* means "He's coming along."

"We believe part of the reason why *with* can appear as both a preposition and a particle here in Wisconsin is that many of the immigrant languages brought to Wisconsin such as German, Dutch and Danish have their version of *with* as a particle," wrote Thomas Purnell, Eric Raimy, and Joseph Salmons in their book *Wisconsin Talk: Linguistic Diversity in the Badger State*. "To put it another way, when immigrants arrived in Wisconsin and began to learn English, they sometimes just directly translated what they wanted to word by word. If this type of translation gets close enough to work within a community, then the construction will be adopted. We can see this type of affect with a few other words in Wisconsin, too. Both the words *yet* and *once* have Wisconsin-specific uses in sentences, such as 'Get me a beer *once* as long as you're up *yet*,' in Lou and Peter Berryman's folk song 'Squirrelly Valley.' As in the *come with* example, we believe we can trace these to the language of German immigrants again because a word-by-word translation from German to English produces these types of sentences."

(Lou and Peter Berryman are a Madison-based duo who, needless to say, play accordion and have performed on *A Prairie Home Companion*.)

"Get me a beer once" doesn't mean "Get me one beer" or "Get me a beer one time." Once is a translation of *mal*, which means "a point in time," and is used to sound less demanding. It's like saying, "Could you get me a beer when you have a chance?"

"Yet comes from *noch*, which means both 'still' and 'yet,'" according to *Wisconsin Talk*. "In this instance, German immigrants used 'yet' to cover all the meanings of 'noch,' and other Wisconsinites picked it up."

Wisconsin is the linguistic crossroads of the Midwest, the only state in which Inland North, Midland, and North Central are spoken. The Northern Cities Vowel Shift is strong in the eastern part of the state, with its connections to Chicago and the Great Lakes. Southwestern Wisconsin, settled by Illinois farmers, is a salient of the Midland dialect region. The North Country speaks North Central, with its trademark interjections of "yah" and "hey dere." Dialect maps show a boundary cutting through Manitowoc

County. The Netflix series *Making a Murderer*, about Steven Avery, a man falsely imprisoned for rape, then rearrested for murder two years after his release, takes place there. The police, judges and prosecutors in the lakefront county seat of Manitowoc speak with urbanized Inland North accents, while the rural Averys are pure North Central, with "deys," "dats," "ya knows" and drawn-out, monophthongal "o"s. The subjects' accents reinforce the series's theme of social class's role in the justice system.

YOOPANESE AND RAYNCHER

" So, ah, I gotta take a shore and then I'll be over to your hoase in aboat an oar, eh."

That was the Flivv, my freshman hall mate at the University of Michigan, telling a friend he needed to take a shower, and would be over at his house in an hour. We called him the Flivv because he came from Kingsford, the Upper Peninsula charcoal-making town whose high school teams are nicknamed the Flivvers. Imitating his Yooper (from "U.P.'er") accent was a popular amusement on the third floor of Alice Lloyd Hall.

Few places in America speak a dialect more distinct from the rest of their state as the U.P., but few places are more remote. Until the Mackinac Bridge opened in 1957, only a ferry transported travelers between Michigan's two peninsulas. It was easier to get there from Ontario or Wisconsin, so naturally, the U.P. developed a pattern of speech that more closely resembled those northern neighbors'. Yoopanese, as it is called, is marked by the use of "eh" and "youse," Canadian raising of vowels, turning *th* into *d*, and a cot-caught merger with a broad *o*. Its lexicon includes such terms as "pank," for patting down snow, "chook" for hat, and "Holy wah!" as an exclamation of surprise. These are all unknown to "trolls"— downstaters who live under the (Mackinac) bridge.

The western U.P., the stronghold of Yoopanese, contains the only counties in the U.S. where Finns are the dominant ethnic group. They arrived in the late nineteenth century to work in the copper mines, and spoke a non-Indo-European language that has nothing in common with English. Had the Finns emigrated to New York, they would have adopted the local speech patterns, adding little of their own. Instead, they arrived in a remote region where they had limited contact with other English speakers, save the mine bosses and the Cornish miners who had preceded them. For reasons of geography and the difficulty of learning an unrelated language, the U.P.'s Finns clung to their ancestral tongue longer than most immigrants. (Finlandia University in Hancock, Mich., is one of only a handful of American institutions of higher learning with a Finnish studies program.) As an isolated community in a strange land, the Finns had to work out their own version of English. As a result, Finnish was such an important influence on Yoopanese that the dialect is also called "Finglish."

Take, for example, my classmate's pronunciation of "shower." Stressing the initial vowel sound is a feature of Finnish, which overwhelmed the American English tendency to pronounce *ow* as a diphthong. Finnish also lacks the *th* sound, so pronouncing "them," "there," and "through" as "dem," "dere," and "t'rough" is the source of much U.P. humor. A band called Da Yoopers recorded a song called "Second Week of Deer Camp." (It's da second week of deer camp/ And all da guys are here/ We drink, play cards and shoot da bull/ But never shoot no deer.") Michigan actor Jeff Daniels wrote and produced the movie *Escanaba in Da Moonlight*, about a "buckless Yooper" who has never killed a deer. In the 1980s, a "Say Yah to Da U.P., Eh" bumper sticker appeared on cars all over the state, as a peninsular response to the era's "Say Yes to Michigan" campaign.

Other immigrant groups also influenced Yoopanese. The Flivv's rendering of "hour" as "oar" and "about" as "aboat" are examples of "Canadian raising," in which words are pronounced higher in the mouth than in General American English. Despite the U.P.'s proximity to Canada, however, that *o* vowel is more likely to have come from Swedish or German, which pronounces "boat" as "boot." The crisp Yooper *r*, pronounced far back in the mouth ("MAR-ket" for "Marquette"), comes from Cornish speech. And then of course, there's "eh," which one scholar of Yoopanese believes is derived from the French-Canadian *hein*.

The tapping out of the copper mines, which forced Yoopers to leave the peninsula for jobs and education, and the building of the Mackinac Bridge, which connected it by road to the rest of the state, led to a heightened consciousness of Yoopanese's distinctiveness, and an embrace of the dialect as a totem of local pride. For decades, U.P. high schools didn't even compete against the Lower Peninsula in sports, because of the travel difficulties. A previously peninsular people were suddenly exposed to an outside world in which their accents distinguished them as Up North rubes—as the Flivv discovered in Ann Arbor. As happened in Pittsburgh after the steel crisis, this led to both dialect leveling—schoolchildren were instructed not to say "dat" and "dose"—and a nostalgic embrace of local argot. The term "Yooper" only dates to 1979, when increasing regional awareness inspired the *Escanaba Daily News* to hold a contest to name inhabitants of the U.P. Linguist Kathryn Remlinger interviewed a Yooper who became acutely self-conscious about his accent after enrolling at the State Police Academy in Lansing: "They asked me about the way I talk and all that. If everybody talks like me who are up here."

The dialect of Minnesota's Iron Range—called "Da Raynch" by its natives—has a history and phonology similar to Yoopanese. The Iron Range was also settled during the nineteenth-century mining boom, by a melting pot of immigrants with a heavy dollop of Finns, and the Rangers were isolated within their mother state by geography and occupation. Up in Minnesota's Arrowhead region, northwest of Duluth, the Range is even today beyond the reach of any interstate highway. Its largest settlement is Hibbing, population 16,000 and best known as the hometown of musician Bob Dylan.

"In the 1800s, the Iron Range had been ignored by westward-migrating Americans looking for farmland because of the dense forests, rocky land and foreboding blizzards," wrote University of Minnesota-Duluth professor Michael D. Linn in the essay "The Origin and Development of the Iron Range Dialect in Northern Minnesota." "As a result, there was no base of English-speaking residents in the area where the rich iron ore deposits were discovered and began to be mined in the 1890s. When the mines were first being developed, there was a large number of non-English speaking immigrants working for a small number of English-speaking bosses. At this time the workers created a foreign or immigrant workers' speech, not unlike that of a plantation pidgin. Like pidgin speakers, these immigrants were actively excluded from the social life of the English-speaking supervisors by the caste system of the locations."

Mining wasn't slavery, but the linguistic result was similar. Just as slaves from different African empires had to figure out how to speak to each other in their new country's language, a Finn, a Croatian, and an Italian thrown together on a work team had only English as a common means of communication. To discourage labor organizing, mine bosses deliberately mixed workers of different nationalities, and did not offer English classes. (Plantation owners had done the same thing, to prevent slaves from plotting revolts.) This led, then, to sentences without "to be," such as, "He late" and, "Where you at?"—a feature also found in African American Vernacular English. It also led to a lack of verb endings—"We stay 'til we move here." Because Finnish lacks prepositions, miners would say "Let's go Dulut'." Best became "bestest," and words were placed out of order: "You play with five cards just."

Sara Schmelzer Loss, an Iron Range native, wrote a doctoral dissertation on the long-distance reflexive use of "himself" in Iron Range English. On the Iron Range, the sentence "Jill said that

Hillary believes in herself" can mean "Jill said that Hillary believes in her." The Iron Range is Minnesota's Minnesota. Even as the rest of the country mocks the *Fargo* accent, flatland Minnesotans make fun of Rangers for compressing "did you eat?" into "jeet?" As a result, young people who leave the Range for the University of Minnesota adopt a standard North Central accent. Even older residents limit their use of "Rayncher" to other Rangers, as a way of showing off their native status and expressing community solidarity against outsiders.

"There are things that only older generations are doing," Loss says. "If you're older, you're more likely not to say the preposition. I can't even say 'Let's go Dulut" with a straight face. Very old people I've heard say it with a straight face. I think a lot of where we change our speech is to be more like other parts of Minnesota and Wisconsin. It's a process where you say something, and other people make fun of it."

Although their grammar is perfectly correct English, prominent modern Iron Rangers still maintain distinctive pronunciations. Former Gov. Rudy Perpich, from Hibbing, and state Sen. Tom Rukavina, from Virginia, both say (or said, in Perpich's case) "aboot" for "about," "tok" for "talk," "knooo" for "know," "tree" for "three" and "cawledge" for "college." (The pronunciations are similar to those of Michigan State University basketball coach Tom Izzo, a Yooper from Iron Mountain, Mich.) Calling the Iron Range "Da Raynch" is an example of final obstruent devoicing, which was carried over from immigrant languages.

"A lot of 'voiced' sounds (ones pronounced with your vocal cord vibrating) are produced without the vocal cords vibrating so they sound voiceless in Iron Range (and some other Midwestern varieties)," Loss says. "Therefore, it's not just 'j' that can sound like 'ch'—but also 'z' that can sound like 's' and 'g' that can sound like 'k.' Devoicing obstruents at the ends of words is a process we see in a lot of languages—German, Russian, Serbo-Croatian."

(Pronouncing final *s* as "sss" rather than "z" is common throughout the North Central region.)

North Country captures this by having a character call a judge a "chudge." Loss also hears the devoiced obstruent in "Blowin' in the Wind," when Bob Dylan sings "How many yearsss can some people exist, before they're allowed to be free?"

Accurate or not, *Fargo* has fixed the Minnesota accent so well in the nation's mind that when Sarah Palin delivered her vice presidential acceptance speech (in St. Paul), journalists commented on her "*Fargo* accent." This was not far off base. Alaska's Matanuska-Susitna Valley, where Palin grew up, was settled during the Depression by farm families from Minnesota, Wisconsin, and Michigan, transplanted there by the Federal Emergency Relief Administration. For better or for worse, Minnesotan is now the most recognizable form of Midwestern speech, a status furthered by *Fargo*'s FX television spinoff. Once, far outside the Midwest, I got a haircut from a barber who heard my Midwestern accent, and asked if I was from Minnesota. He was a fan of the TV show. I told him he should go to Brainerd to see and hear the real thing. The snowmobiling is great there, too.

KEY FEATURES OF THE NORTH CENTRAL DIALECT

- "Cot-caught merger": in North Central, both words sound like "cahht." "Don't get cahht ridin' your snowmobile without a helmet."

- Monophthongal o: the compression of a two-stepped vowel into a single sound, resulting in pronunciations such as "knooo" for "know."

- "Yah" and "you bet" to signal agreement.

- Devoiced obstruents, especially pronouncing final s as "sss" rather than "z."

- "By" to indicate location: "I'm down by the bookstore."

- Among far northern speakers, "eh" as an interjection to invite a response, or confirm a listener's attentiveness.

A glossary of

MIDWESTERN TERMS

BUFFALO

The 190: Buffalonians refer to their highways by number, not name, and always prefix them with "the." The 190 is a highway running along the Niagara River, out to the Falls. The 290 is a beltway around the city.

Beef on Weck: A sandwich consisting of soggy tissues of rare roast beef packed inside a *Kummelweck*—a Kaiser roll studded with pretzel salt and caraway seeds. Best served with horseradish sauce, which makes every mouthful sweet, salty, and pungent. Buffalo was once a big beer town, and beef on weck was popularized by German brewers looking to parch their customers.

Buff State: Buffalo State College, a State University of New York (SUNY) campus. Not to be confused with the much larger University of Buffalo.

Bumper Skating: Grabbing the back of a car and sliding down an icy street. Also known as pogeying, skeeching, or skedding.

Butter Lamb: A lamb sculpted in butter which decorates Easter tables in Catholic homes. According to the late Dorothy Malczewski, who introduced the Polish tradition to Buffalo, "[T]he Butter Lamb symbolizes the sacrifice of the Lamb of God in the Eucharist. The Malczewski Butter Lamb comes…with a red 'alleluia' flag signifying peace on earth, and a red ribbon signifying the Blood of Christ."

Caz Creek: Cazenovia Creek, a tributary of the Buffalo River. Scajaquada Creek is known as Scaj Creek.

The Chip Strip: Chippewa Street in downtown Buffalo, once so sleazy that "I saw your mama on Chippewa Street" was a schoolyard insult; now an upscale entertainment district.

Deli: A convenience store selling pop, snacks, and sundries, often owned by a Middle Eastern immigrant.

Elevator Alley: A stretch of grain elevators on the Buffalo River. Abandoned when the St. Lawrence Seaway allowed freighters to bypass Buffalo, the elevators have been embraced as a destination for kayak tours and screens for nighttime light shows.

Fastnacht: A flat, fried pastry sprinkled with cinnamon or sugar, served before Lent. A German version of the Polish packzi.

Garbage Plate: Traditionally, a base of home fries and macaroni salad, topped with red hots, a cheeseburger patty, mustard, horseradish sauce, and chili. The Garbage Plate originated at Nick Tahou Hots in Rochester, and is now served to late-night drunks all over western New York. Although the base is essential, a Garbage Plate can also be topped with sausage, eggs, steak, chicken tenders, haddock, and fried ham.

Genny: Genesee Cream Ale. Western New York's hometown beer, brewed in Rochester. Also known as Genny Scream or Green Death, after the color of the can.

"I'm Going Over the Border": Going to Canada, usually to a casino or the "Canadian ballet," one of the strip clubs in every Canadian border town. International day trippers may also say, "I'm crossing the bridge."

Lake Effect Snow: Snow generated when cold air passes over warmer lake waters, causing them to evaporate and form clouds. Located at the eastern end of 241-mile-long Lake Erie, Buffalo is the frequent repository of such precipitation. In January 1977, a blizzard piled snowdrifts thirty feet high, turning Buffalo into a national symbol of hard winters. Buffalo annually competes for the Golden Snowball, awarded to the snowiest city in western New York. Syracuse, which averages 110 inches, and Rochester, with 88, usually beat 83-inch-a-year Buffalo.

McKinley's Curse: On September 6, 1901, anarchist Leon Czolgosz shot William McKinley in the abdomen as the president shook hands inside the Temple of Music at Buffalo's Pan-American Exposition. Eight days later, McKinley died of his wound. At the time, Buffalo was the eighth largest city in the U.S., and was said to have the most millionaires. The city's subsequent decline has been blamed on a curse deriving from the assassination. So has the failure of Buffalo sports teams to win a championship since the Bills' 1965 AFL title.

No Goal: Along with "WIDE RIGHT," a cry of sporting futility. In game six of the 1999 Stanley Cup finals, Dallas Stars forward Brett Hull scored the Cup-winning goal in triple overtime. Sabres fans have always maintained the goal should have been waved off, because Hull's skate was in the crease in front of goalie Dominik Hasek. In 2014, a Lululemon store in Buffalo spelled out "Wide Right" and "No Goal" in floor tile mosaic, but covered it up after sports fans protested these reminders of their most painful memories.

Polish Patio: A screened-in garage for sitting out in the summer.

The Queen City: Buffalo's original nickname, because it was the second-largest city in New York State and the largest on the Great Lakes. Cincinnati also calls itself the Queen City, but Buffalo did it first. Also known as Nickel City, because buffaloes once appeared on the obverse of nickels.

The Ralph: Ralph Wilson Stadium, home of the Bills.

The Southtowns: The southern suburbs of Buffalo, including Hamburg, East Aurora and Blasdell. THE RALPH is in Orchard Park.

Sponge Candy: Milk chocolate bites filled with caramelized sugar.

Texas Red Hot: A charcoal grilled hot dog, usually served with mustard, onions, and a special sauce concocted by the Greek who owns the joint.

"Wide Right": In the 1990s, the Buffalo Bills went to four straight Super Bowls—and lost them all. The most painful was XXV. Trailing the New York Giants 20-19 with eight seconds left, the Bills sent in placekicker Scott Norwood, who shanked the potential game winner "wide right" in the words of announcer Al Michaels. The missed kick figures in the plot of the movie *Buffalo '66*: Vincent Gallo's character, Billy, had to serve another man's five-year prison sentence so a bookie would forgive him the $10,000 he lost betting on the game. After his release, he tries to kill "Scott Wood," the kicker who missed the field goal.

Wings: The rest of the world knows them as Buffalo wings, but in Buffalo, they're just wings. First served at the Anchor Bar on March 4, 1964, when bartender Dominic Bellisimo asked his mother to prepare a meal for his friends. She deep-fried chicken wings, an appendage of the bird that usually went into the stockpot, and basted them with a sweet sauce. Wings are best eaten with bleu cheese and celery.

"You're Going to Father Baker's!": When Buffalo children of past generations misbehaved, they were threatened with consignment to a now-closed orphanage founded by Father Nelson Baker, the Catholic priest who also built Our Lady of Victory Basilica in Lackawanna.

THE GREAT LAKES

The Academy: The Great Lakes Maritime Academy in Traverse City, Mich., which trains engineers and officers for freighters. If you don't want to work your way up as a HAWSEPIPE, enroll here.

The Beach: Dry land. The world is divided into sailors and "people on the beach."

The Big Blow: The second week of November is the most perilous time of the year on the Great Lakes, as cold fronts from Canada collide with warm air from the Gulf of Mexico, producing ferocious storms. None was more destructive than "The Big Blow," which raged from November 7 to 10, 1913, sinking a dozen ships and drowning nearly 300 sailors.

Boat: A ship. Sailors refer to their work as "going out on the boats."

Boat Nerd: The nautical equivalent of trainspotters, boat nerds travel the Great Lakes with copies of *Know Your Ships*, checking off every freighter they see. They wear T-shirts with pictures of their favorite boats. Can be seen on the observation platform at the Soo Locks, or Vantage Point in Port Huron, Mich. Inspired the Great Lakes shipping website boatnerd.com.

Calcite: Sailors' name for Rogers City, Mich., which has the world's most productive limestone quarry. The Michigan Limestone and Chemical Co. built a fleet to transport the limestone to steel mills, beginning Rogers City's nautical tradition. In 1958, one of its boats, the *Carl F. Bradley*, sank on Lake Michigan, drowning 33 local men.

Coast Guard City, U.S.A.: Grand Haven, Mich., which holds an annual festival in honor of its Coast Guard installation.

Esky: Escanaba, a busy TACONITE port on the Lake Michigan shore of Michigan's Upper Peninsula.

The Fitz: The *Edmund Fitzgerald*, which on November 10, 1975, became the last freighter to sink on the Great Lakes. The disaster was memorialized by Gordon Lightfoot's ballad "The Wreck of the Edmund Fitzgerald," and is commemorated every year by a ceremony at the Great Lakes Shipwreck Museum in Whitefish Point, Mich., which is attended by crew members' families, and, sometimes, Lightfoot himself.

Footer: One of the thirteen thousand-foot-long BOATS plying the Great Lakes. Sightings are coveted by BOAT NERDS. The longest is the *Paul R. Tregurtha*, which at 1,013 feet holds title "Queen of the Lakes." The size of LAKERS is limited by the length of the 1,200-foot-long Poe Lock in Sault Ste. Marie, Mich.

Hawsepipe: A mate or captain who began his career as a deckhand, rather than attending THE ACADEMY. The term is derived from the pipe through which the anchor chain passes. "Climbing the hawsepipe" is analogous to climbing the ranks from the bottom.

Kitchi Gami: Ojibway name for Lake Superior, meaning, roughly, "Big Water." In his epic poem *The Song of Hiawatha*, Henry Wadsworth Longfellow transcribed it as Gitchee Gumee: "By the shores of Gitchee Gumee, by the shining big sea water, stood the wigwam of Nokomis…"

Laker: A BOAT that sails only on the Great Lakes.

The Mac: The Chicago to Mackinac Race, a 333-mile sailing competition. First held in 1898, it's the world's oldest freshwater sailing event.

The Only Floating Zip Code in the United States: 48222, which is assigned to the *J. W. Westcott II*, a boat that delivers mail and supplies to passing freighters from its dock at the foot of 24th Street in Detroit.

The Playpen: A no-wake zone off Oak Street Beach in Chicago, mostly enclosed by breakwaters, in which pleasure craft drop anchor each summer for drinking, drugs, loud music, and other forms of nautical debauchery.

Salty: An oceangoing ship that reaches the Great Lakes via the St. Lawrence Seaway. Often delivers steel and takes home grain. Salty crews spend their time on the BEACH buying jeans and electronic gadgets, which are much less expensive in the U.S. than back home in Latvia or Poland.

Shoulder Seasons: The spring, after the ice breaks up, and the fall, before it re-forms, when there is limited shipping and boating activity on the Lakes.

Up the Street: Where sailors go to drink. "We're going up the street" means "We're going to a bar."

Z Card: A credential issued by the Coast Guard, entitling the bearer to work as a merchant seaman.

ILLINOIS

16-inch: Uniquely Chicago brand of slow-pitch softball that caught on during the Great Depression for two very practical reasons: a bigger, softer ball didn't travel as far as the standard 12-incher, so it couldn't be hit out of tiny urban parks. And it could be caught barehanded, by fielders who couldn't afford gloves. Each summer, Chicago emergency rooms see a spike in walk-in patients with jammed or broken fingers, most of them still wearing their softball jerseys.

American Bottom: A fertile alluvial floodplain on the eastern bank of the Mississippi River, from Alton to Kaskaskia. The American Bottom supported Cahokia, a city of Native American mound builders who developed the most advanced pre-Columbian civilization in the United States, peaking at a population of 20,000 in the thirteenth century. After Cahokia's decline, the American Bottom was settled by French missionaries, who founded Kaskaskia, the state's first capital. The region got its name after the War of Independence, when Americans began settling there, and wanted to distinguish themselves from the Spanish territory across the river. Bounded on the east by bluffs, the American Bottom is susceptible to flooding, so it quickly lost its position as Illinois's population center. However, today it is coterminous with METRO EAST, and its soil produces two-thirds of the nation's horseradish.

Below the Hill: The METRO EAST cities west of the ridge that forms the AMERICAN BOTTOM, including East St. Louis. Sometimes used as a euphemism for the area's African American communities.

Burgoo: A pioneer stew originally made with squirrel, venison, and whatever vegetables the prairie's first settlers could grow. Every

October, Utica holds a Burgoo Festival, at which volunteers spend all day over a wood fire, mixing a concoction of beef, carrots, potatoes, hominy, celery, tomatoes, cabbage, onions, and peppers. (It's still legal to kill a squirrel and eat it, but not to serve it to someone else.)

Bungalow Belt: The brick bungalow is the prototypical working-class Chicago dwelling, especially common in areas far from the lake that were developed during the city's rapid expansion in the nineteen teens and twenties. "Bungalow Belt" is a politico-sociological term for the socially conservative, racially segregated white neighborhoods of the Northwest and Southwest sides, which in the 1980s united in opposition to Harold Washington, the city's first black mayor.

Carbondalay: Faux-pretentious pronunciation of Carbondale, home to Southern Illinois University, where a lot of Chicago-area students are slumming it 300 miles from home. Like calling Target "Tar-zhay."

Cheeseheads: Wisconsinites, who embrace the nickname by wearing foam wedges shaped and colored to look like cheddar on their heads at Green Bay Packers games. Chicago Bears fans respond by wearing cheese graters on their heads.

Cheese Toastie: A grilled cheese sandwich.

Chiberia: Chicago, under a polar vortex.

Chi-cah-go vs. Chi-caw-go: So how exactly do you pronounce Chicago? The Daley family says "Chi-caw-go," which ought to settle it, since being more Chicago than a Daley is like being more Catholic than the pope. "If you hear someone say Chi-cah-go, ask them where they're from," says a local historian who grew up on the EAST SIDE in the 1950s and '60s. "Chi-cah-go sounds like more of a transplant." Chicago has always been a city of transplants, attracting immigrants and the ambitious; their pronunciation seems to be prevailing. Barack Obama, who grew up in Hawaii, began his 2008 presidential acceptance speech "Hello, Chi-cah-go!" The future of Chicago belongs to Chi-cah-goans.

Chilli: A spicy stew of tomatoes, beef, and beans. The spelling is probably derived from the first four letters of Illinois. A chilli mac is chilli served over spaghetti. Available at all Steak 'n' Shake restaurants.

Chiraq: Portmanteau of Chicago and Iraq, meant to compare the parts of the city plagued by gang violence with a Middle Eastern war zone. Sometimes called Chiraq, Drillinois, after the DRILL music the mayhem inspired. Spike Lee's 2015 movie *Chi-Raq* is a *Lysistrata* take-off about women who try to stop a gang war by withholding sex from their boyfriends. The term was coined by rapper King Louie, who was shot in the head while sitting in a parked car in 2015.

Clout: Political influence used to evade rules that must be followed by the less well-connected. Possessors can obtain no-bid contracts, police department promotions, admissions to selective high schools, and other favors. Both a noun and a verb. A political sponsor is a clout (formerly known by the politically incorrect term "Chinaman"). The late newspaper columnist Mike Royko provided proper uses of the term in a 1973 column: "Hey, Charlie, I see you made foreman. Who's clouting for you?" Or, "Ever since my clout died, they've been making me work a full eight hours. I've never worked an eight-hour week before."

Cooler by the Lake: Phrase used in weather reports to describe the microclimate that makes Lake Michigan beaches up to ten degrees colder than the rest of Chicago. "Eighty-two degrees at Midway, eighty-three at O'Hare. Cooler by the lake."

Dibs: In Chicago, competition for street parking is fierce, especially in the winter. If you shovel out a space on your block, you call "dibs" by blocking it with lawn chairs, crates, sawhorses, or other cast-off possessions. Became an accepted practice after the 1967 blizzard, which hit the city with 23 inches of snow. Drivers who violate dibs are likely to find key tracks on their paint jobs—or worse.

Downstate: Any part of Illinois SOUTH OF I-80.

Drill: A dark, hardcore iteration of hip-hop that developed in Englewood, a poor African American neighborhood on the South Side. Prominent artists include Chief Keef, Lil Durk, Lil Reese, and King Louie. Lyrics are frequently about street life, and include disses of rival gang members that have led to retaliatory shootings. Coined by Pac Man, a rapper who was shot to death in 2010. Drill groupies are known as "cloutheads."

East Boogie: East St. Louis, a nickname acquired when it still had a vibrant nightlife.

The Edens, the Eisenhower, the Stevenson, the Dan Ryan: Chicagoans refer to expressways by name, not number: "This is your WGN traffic helicopter. GAPERS BLOCK slowing down traffic on the outbound Ike due to an accident near Damen."

I-290: The Eisenhower (or Ike)
I-55: The Stevenson
I-94: The Edens Expressway
I-90: The Kennedy
I-90/94: The Dan Ryan
I-88: The Reagan
I-294: The Tri-State Tollway
I-94 South: The Bishop Ford Freeway (formerly the Calumet Expressway)

Frunchroom: The front room of a bungalow or flat, overlooking the street. The frunchroom contains the family's best furniture, but it's only used to entertain company or open Christmas presents.

Gangway: A sidewalk running through a narrow space between two houses. Cop: "You see where that kid went?" Witness: "Yeah. He ran t'rough da gangway."

Gapers Block: A traffic jam, due to motorists rubbernecking at an accident. Also known as "gaper delay."

Goo-Goo: A derisive term for a political idealist, traditionally used by Roman Catholic regulars to belittle Protestant reformers who wanted to clean up the city's MACHINE, usually by eliminating patronage. Short for "good government."

Gym shoes: Sneakers or athletic shoes.
"What kind of gym shoes did your maa buy you this year?"
"P.F. Flyers!"

The Hawk: A cold wind off Lake Michigan. The term originated in Chicago's African American community, and was brought to the world's attention by smooth R&B balladeer Lou Rawls, who mentioned it in the spoken-word intro to his song "Dead End Street": "The Hawk, the almighty Hawk, the wind…in Chicago, the Hawk not only socks it to you, he socks it through you, like a giant razor blade blowing down the street."

Horseshoe: An open-faced sandwich of ham, turkey, or hamburger on two slices of toast, covered with French fries and smothered in cheese sauce. Invented in Springfield, and second only to Abraham Lincoln as a local icon.

Hunnerts: Every Chicago block encompasses 100 street numbers, measured from the city's zero point at the intersection of State and Madison streets. Thus, Belmont Avenue, which is 32 blocks from Madison, is "thirty-two hunnert north." Irving Park Road is forty blocks from Madison. Many Chicagoans would say it's not "four thousand north" but "forty hunnert north," because one block equals a hunnert, therefore, forty hunnerts.

Italian Beef: The Italian Beef, also known as a "beef sammich" or "I.B.," is a pile of sliced beef packed into a roll, only to prevent it from slipping through your fingers. Order one, and the counterman will ask "Dipped?," meaning dunked in its own juices, and "hot or sweet?" meaning the flavor of the peppers.

The Jewels: Jewel, a popular Chicago-area grocery store chain.

The L: Short for elevated train. Chicago's intra-urban commuter line, which runs above the street in most parts of the city.

La Guiannee: A French New Year's Eve celebration observed in Prairie du Rocher every December 31 since 1722, when the Mississippi Valley was part of a French empire that formed a great crescent from Quebec to New Orleans. A few hours before midnight, carolers begin traveling from house to house, singing and fiddling a traditional French begging song, accepting refreshments—often alcoholic—from those they serenade. La Guiannee originated in medieval France, and Prairie du Rocher is the only American city with a continuous observance dating back to the colonial era.

Little Egypt: Southern Illinois, below Interstate 70. Towns include Thebes, Karnak, and Cairo. Southern Illinois University's mascot is the Saluki, an Egyptian dog breed, and the student newspaper is the

Daily Egyptian. The book *Legends and Lore of Southern Illinois* claims the region got its name after a hard frost in 1831 forced northern Illinois farmers to travel south to buy feed for their livestock. Like the sons of Jacob in the Bible, they were said to be "going down to Egypt for corn." Other theories say it's because the land around the confluence of the Ohio and Mississippi rivers resembles the Nile Delta. Some Southern Illinoisans object to the term Little Egypt because it was also the name of a fan dancer at the 1893 World's Fair, and simply call their home "Egypt."

The Loop: The core of downtown Chicago, so named because it is defined by elevated rail lines that form a rectangle bounded by Lake Street on the north, Wabash Avenue on the east, Van Buren Street on the south, and Wells Street on the west. The term, however, is often applied to a much broader area, and is a synonym for the central business district. The South Loop is a trendy neighborhood far from the L tracks.

Maa: Mother. "If you don't pay me the fi' dollars you owe me, I'll tell yer maa."

Machine: The Cook County Regular Democratic Organization. Founded by Mayor Anton Cermak as a multiethnic political alliance. Reached its maximum efficiency under Richard J. Daley, who served as mayor and party chairman from 1955 until his death in 1976. A rigid hierarchy resembling the Catholic Church, with the mayor as pope, ward committeemen as bishops, and precinct captains as priests, the Machine kept power through patronage, awarding government jobs to ward organizations that got out the vote—a practice that is now illegal, weakening the Machine's effectiveness. The Machine had a powerful attraction for immigrants and newly urbanized blacks who depended on government for jobs, services and holiday meals, but was extremely clannish. When aspiring young politician Abner J. Mikva showed up at a ward office to volunteer in 1948, a heeler famously asked him, "Who sent you?" "Nobody," the young man responded. "We don't want nobody nobody sent," he was told.

Melvina, Paulina, and Lunt: Punch line for the classic Chicago joke, "Name three streets that rhyme with a woman's body part."

Merch: To offer proof. "I saw Bill with Tiffany at the bar and I know she talks to my cousin and I can prove it." "Merch."

Metro East: The trans-Mississippi suburbs of St. Louis, encompassing Madison and St. Clair counties. Includes East St. Louis, Alton, Granite City, Belleville, and Sauget, which was incorporated by Monsanto to evade local environmental regulations, and is now so polluted that a waterless ditch known as Dead Creek is said to glow at night. Sauget's lax laws also enable the Sauget Ballet, a set of sleazy strip clubs popular with St. Louisans.

Out South: The South Side or south suburbs. "Where you stay at?" "Out South. In Harvey."

Pinners: A street game played by flinging a rubber ball against a set of concrete steps or a ledge. If an opposing player catches the rebound, it's an out. Singles, doubles, triples, and home runs are scored if the ball passes predetermined landmarks. Also known as "Three Outs" or "Ledge."

Shampoo Banana: Champaign-Urbana, the twin cities that contain the University of Illinois campus.

Show: Chicagoans don't go to the movies, they go to the show. Radio station WXRT airs a long-running feature called "Going to the Show with the Regular Guy," in which a disc jockey delivers film reviews in an exaggerated Chicago accent.

The Smell of Money: The odor of roasting corn and soybeans emanating from the A.E. Staley and Archer Daniels Midland plants in Decatur. Mention it to a native and he'll respond, "That smells like a paycheck to people who work there," then expect you to stop noticing it.

South of I-80: Interstate 80 is the traditional dividing line between greater Chicago and downstate Illinois. "You're south of I-80 now" is an invitation to informality. Someone who says "I'm from Illinois" probably lives south of I-80. Chicagoans aren't from Illinois. Chicagoans are from Chicago.

Springpatch: Springfield, to the colony of politicians, lobbyists, and journalists who descend on the state capital for legislative sessions. Sometimes shortened to "The Patch."

Trixie: A usually blonde-haired young woman living in Chicago's affluent Lincoln Park neighborhood. Preoccupations include shopping at spendy boutiques, drinking cocktails at the bar associated with her Big Ten college, and summer weekends at the Michigan cottage of boyfriend Chad's parents. In her thirties, Trixie marries Chad and moves to the suburbs, becoming Deerfield Trixie.
T-town: Teutopolis, a small town in Effingham County (also known as "Eff County").

Two Flat and Three Flat: Multi-unit brick apartment buildings (most Chicago structures were built with brick after the Great Fire of 1871) with a common entrance in the vestibule.

Wear the Jacket: During a political scandal, an underling who takes the fall for his boss's misdeeds is said to "wear the jacket." "Jeez, the

Building Department hired a union president's nineteen-year-old son as an inspector. Who's gonna wear the jacket for that?"

"Will It Play in Peoria?": Illinois reflects the nation's demographics more closely than any state. No city embodies that averageness more than Peoria. The phrase "Will it play in Peoria?" originated with vaudeville performers who saw Peorians as an ideal audience test audience for shows. It was popularized by Groucho Marx. Peoria's proverbial Middle Americanness was later put to use by corporate marketers, who tested Pampers, the McRib sandwich, and New Coke there before selling the products nationally.

The Windy City: Nickname for Chicago, which does not refer to THE HAWK, but to the city's capacity for boastfulness and self-promotion. It was first used in an 1876 *Cincinnati Enquirer* headline, when both cities were vying to become capital of the Midwest. A tornado on May 6 of that year provided the *Enquirer* with the opportunity to crack that not only was Chicago's weather full of wind, so were its leading citizens.

The Wild Hundreds: The neighborhood of Roseland, which runs along South Michigan Avenue from 95th Street to 115th Street and is marked by high levels of gang activity.

INDIANA

Barnburner: A close, intense sporting event. This phrase has been adopted by sports announcers nationwide (especially ABC's Keith Jackson), but it originated in Indiana, where early high school basketball games were played in barns.

The Bend: South Bend, which got its name because of its location on the St. Joseph River. The river originates in Michigan, dips into Indiana, then returns to Michigan to empty into Lake Michigan at St. Joseph. Inhabitants of South Bend are known as "Benders."

Bloomingulch: Bloomington, home of Indiana University.

Boiler Up!: Cheer for the Purdue University Boilermakers, whose nickname refers to the fact the school specializes in engineering.

The Brickyard: The Indianapolis Motor Speedway, site of the Indy 500. After two spectators and a mechanic were killed when a car blew a tire and ran off the crushed stone and tar surface during the inaugural weekend of racing in 1909, the tracks' owners paved it with bricks. The bricks were paved over with tarmac in the 1930s, to accommodate faster cars, but the nickname stuck, and a three-foot wide strip of bricks still marks the finish line. As stock car racing eclipsed Indy car racing in popularity, the track began holding the Brickyard 400, one of NASCAR's most lucrative races.

Couple Three: More than one, less than a half dozen. A common Midwestern numerical estimate.

Cutters: Bloomington townies, because they work in the limestone quarry. Introduced to the world by the movie *Breaking Away*, in which a team of locals calling themselves Cutters wins the Little 500, a 50-mile bicycle race held on the cinder track at Indiana University's Bill Armstrong Stadium. (In real life, only IU students are allowed to compete.)

Domer: A student at the University of Notre Dame, after the golden dome of the school's Main Building.

Duneland: The Indiana Dunes and surrounding area, from the Arcelor-Mittal steel mill to Michigan City. Indiana's remaining Lake Michigan dunes were declared a national lakeshore in 1966, to protect them from the encroachments of the steel industry. A spot for swimming, hang-gliding, and hiking.

Dyngus Day: A gluttonous post-Lenten festival celebrated for over 80 years by the Polish Catholic community of northern Indiana, and by anyone else there who likes to eat. Begins with a pancake breakfast and ends with Polish sausage suppers at Elks Lodges, union halls, Knights of Columbus halls, and political party headquarters. Dyngus Day has political overtones, because it occurs close to Indiana's May primary, making Dyngus celebrations a must-visit for candidates. On Dyngus Day 1968, Robert Kennedy spoke to 6,000 supporters at South Bend's West Side Democratic & Civic Club, contributing to his primary victory. The club still calls itself "The Home of Dyngus Day."

Euchre: Euchre (pronounced YOO-ker) is a partnered bidding game similar to bridge, but it's bridge for people who don't want to deal with all 52 cards. Played with only the nines, tens, aces, and face cards. After trump is called, the cards skid across the table until one team wins three tricks. The game was brought to the Midwest from Germany, and, like the complacent Teutonic farmers who popularized it, never traveled outside the region. Its terminology is rustic: bad cards are "a farmer's hand." The highest card, the jack of trumps, is "the right bower." A team one point from victory is "in the barn" (and announces it by mooing). After winning a round, a player may interlace his fingers, point thumbs downward, and command his partner to "milk me!" Pulling the thumbs is a farm belt high five. Euchre is played extensively on Midwestern college campuses, because what else is there do in South Bend on a Tuesday night in February?

Fricassee: A heavy soup containing chicken, beef, bacon, Navy beans, potatoes, onions, and tomatoes. Also, a fundraiser or social event at which said soup is served. "The annual St. Peter Lutheran Church Fall Fricassee will be held from noon to 1 p.m. on Saturday. Fricassee, hamburgers and brats will be served and there will be a pie sale."—*Vincennes Sun-Commercial.*

Hoo Hoo Hoo Hoosiers!: A cheer for the IU basketball team.

Hoosier: A demonym applied to all things Indiana. IU's sports teams are the Hoosiers, the scratch-off tickets are from the Hoosier Lottery, and Indianapolis Colts used to play in the Hoosier Dome. As an essay distributed by the Indiana Historic Bureau points out, "It is one of the oldest nicknames and has had a wider acceptance than most. True there are the Buckeyes of Ohio, the Suckers of Illinois and the Tarheels of North Carolina—but none of these has had the popular usage accorded Hoosier." The word dates back to the 1830s, but no one is certain how it originated. One theory suggests it's because Indiana settlers answered their doors, "Who's yere?" Another says it's because Indiana rivermen always succeeding in "hushing" their opponents in fistfights. Indiana poet James Whitcomb Riley, who observed the state's brawling spirit, jokingly theorized it was because so many ears were torn off in tussles that people would point at a missing appendage on the floor and ask, "Who's ear?"

Hoosier Hysteria: The excitement that sweeps the state during the high school basketball tournament. Portrayed in the movie *Hoosiers*, which fictionalized the story of tiny Milan High School's 1954 victory over Muncie Central, a four-time state champion. Basketball was introduced to Indiana by Rev. Nicholas McKay, a graduate of the International YMCA Training School in Springfield, Mass., where Dr. James A. Naismith invented the game, and has been a statewide obsession ever since. The term "Final Four" was first used in the 1930s to refer to the high school tourney's semi-finalists. The saying goes, "In 49 states it's just basketball…but this is Indiana!"

The Jack: The Joyce Athletic and Convocation Center, home of Notre Dame basketball. Its double-humped white roof is said to resemble a brassiere.

Michiana: Portmanteau of "Michigan" and "Indiana." Sometimes used narrowly to refer to the Lake Michigan shore between Michigan City, Ind., and Union Pier, Mich., but in fact denotes a much larger area centered on South Bend. Vacation spot for Chicagoans, including Oprah Winfrey, who owned a farm near LaPorte.

Naptown: Indianapolis, because it includes the word "nap," and because, for a major city, it's exceedingly colorless and boring. Also known as Indy, Circle City, and End-of-No-Place.

Ooey Pooey: Indiana University-Purdue University in Indianapolis, abbreviated as IUPUI. Read that as a word, and it sounds like "ooey pooey."

Pitch In: A potluck supper. Also known as a "carry in." "Lyons Senior Citizens Center will have our pitch-in dinner so bring in a covered dish and join us there will be bingo after lunch"—*Greene County Daily World*.

Da Region: The Calumet Region, named for the Calumet River, and encompassing the industrial cities of Lake County: Hammond, Whiting, East Chicago, Munster, Griffith, and Gary. Described as "an urban barnacle on the underside of Chicago," it's a smoky, odoriferous landscape of steel mills and oil refineries, so at odds with small-town Indiana that its inhabitants are called "Region Rats," after millrat, a pejorative term for a steelworker. Remarking on Indiana's reputation as a red state, a Region Rat once said, "That's those Colts fans. Up here, we root for da Bears and da Democrats."

Sugar Cream Pie: The official state pie, this custard pie sprinkled with nutmeg was introduced by Amish and Shakers too hard pressed to afford fruit filling. Also known as "Hoosier Pie."

Smick Chick: A student at St. Mary's College (SMC), the all-female sister school of Notre Dame.

Stoplight City: Evansville or Kokomo, depending on where you're stuck at a red light. Neither city is on an interstate, so driving through town means encountering traffic signals, an inconvenience complained about by both travelers and locals.

Tenderloin: A pork fritter sandwich, served in every diner and grill. It's such a Hoosier culinary staple that when Mitch Daniels was campaigning for governor, he ate one in every county. For more cholesterol, fat, and calories, ask for a "breaded loin."

Touchdown Jesus: A stained glass portrait of Jesus Christ on the Notre Dame library, so called because it can be viewed through a set of goalposts in the football stadium.

UrbEx: Urban Exploration, the hobby of breaking into and photographing abandoned buildings. Gary is a popular destination for this Rust Belt amusement, particularly because of City Methodist Church, whose caved-in roof opens the sanctuary to the sky, and Gary Screw & Bolt, where a ten-foot-high drift of work clothes molders on an empty shop floor. Unlike Detroit, which regards Urban Exploration as RUIN PORN, Gary sees it as a tourist opportunity, and wants to turn City Methodist into a "ruin garden" where UrbExers can gawk safely.

WOWOland: The listening area of 50,000-watt WOWO in Fort Wayne, which in 1930 became the first radio station to broadcast a basketball game.

Zoy: The Zoy Run, a grueling 15K cross-country race originally contested in Indiana Dunes State Park. The name comes from an exclamation of exhilaration uttered by Chesterton High School's runners, the "Barefoot Boys of the Dunes" who outran flatlanders in state meets. Cresting a dune, they shouted "zoy!" Banned from the park, because too many runners were trampling the dunes, the Zoy Run was succeeded by Bride of Zoy, elsewhere on the lakeshore.

IOWA

Beans: Soy beans, Iowa's other staple crop, after corn.

The Bix: A seven-mile road race held each July in Davenport. Named for jazz trumpeter Bix Beiderbecke, a QUAD CITIES native. The race was validated in the running community by the participation of marathon champions Bill Rodgers and Joan Benoit Samuelson, who are honored with statues near the riverfront.

The Boats: Iowa was the first state to legalize riverboat gambling, in 1989, and now has fourteen floating casinos on the Missouri and Mississippi rivers. "I'm going to the boats" means the speaker is about to lose a lot of money.

"Born, Bred, Corn Fed": A native Iowan.

Butter Cow: Every summer since 1911, a cow sculpted from 600 pounds of butter has gone on display at the state fair in Des Moines. Butter sculpture is a peculiarly Iowan art form: over the years, the cow had been accompanied by the father and daughter from Iowa painter Grant Wood's *American Gothic*, Elvis Presley, a Harley-Davidson, and a 2,000-pound rendition of the Last Supper.

Butter on a Stick: A stick of butter dipped in cinnamon-honey batter, deep-fried, and glazed. Introduced at the state fair in 2011, in honor of the BUTTER COW's centennial.

The Caucus: Every four years, Iowa holds the nation's first presidential nominating caucus. Loved by some, because it's the only time the rest of the nation pays attention to Iowa, and because any Iowan can meet a candidate in person. Loathed by others, because of incessant TV ads, mailers, phone calls, and door knocks from campaign volunteers. Hamburg Inn, an Iowa City diner, holds a "Coffee Bean Caucus," inviting customers to drop a bean into a jar bearing the name of their favorite candidate.

Cedar Rancid: Cedar Rapids, to its disaffected youth. Also known as Cedar Crapids.

Dirty Burge: Burge Hall, a University of Iowa dormitory notorious for drinking, loud music and hookups.

Dutch Letter: A Christmas treat in Dutch-settled northwest Iowa. Dutch Letters are S-shaped pastries filled with almond paste and studded with sugar crystals.

East Coast: The Mississippi River

The Full Grassley: Visiting all ninety-nine counties, as Sen. Chuck Grassley does each year.

Hoover-ball: A volleyball-like game in which three-player teams toss a six-pound medicine ball over a net. Invented by a White House physician to help the stout Herbert Hoover lose weight. The Hoover Presidential Library in the 31st president's hometown of West Branch holds an annual Hoover-ball tournament.

Hunnerd: Hundred, as heard in descriptions of wrestling weight classes. "Tyler Crisman will be wrestling at a hunnerd and forty-three pounds today." Iowans are mad about wrestling. High school results take up a full page in the sports section, and matches are broadcast on radio. Under coach Dan Gable, a Waterloo native and Olympic medalist, the Iowa Hawkeyes won 15 NCAA wrestling titles.

I Oughta Went Around: What "Iowa" stands for, according to residents of Illinois, Missouri, Nebraska, South Dakota, Minnesota, and Wisconsin. Alternately, "Idiots Out Walking Around."

I-Cubs: The Iowa Cubs, the Chicago Cubs' AAA farm team in Des Moines.

Kybo: A porta-john.

Loose Meat Sandwich: Another term for a Maid-Rite, a dry, crumbly beef sandwich invented in Muscatine in 1926, and now sold at diners across the Midwest.

Magic Mountain: Texas toast topped with ground beef, French fries, and cheese sauce. Served at Ross' Restaurant in Bettendorf. When hot chili and onions are added, it becomes a Volcano.

Mettwurst: A ring sausage cold-smoked in the Plattdeutsch communities of western Iowa. Since cold smoking is not a USDA approved form of sausage preparation, mettwurst is available only at farmers' homes, and a February church supper hosted by St. John's Lutheran in Mineola.

Muscatine Melons: Juicy melons grown in the sandy alluvial soil of Muscatine Island, a peninsula between Muscatine Slough and the Mississippi. Sold by truck farmers from stands along Highway 61. So renowned is the fruit that Muscatine calls itself "Melon City."

Quad Cities: A bi-state metropolitan area that spans the Mississippi River, with Rock Island and Moline on the Illinois side, Davenport and Bettendorf on the Iowa side. In the *Saturday Night Live* skit "Fred Garvin, Male Prostitute," which takes place in a Moline motel room, Dan Aykroyd plays a polyester-clad gigolo who services "the entire Quad Cities area" while looking like a member of the Elks Club. Abbreviated as "QC" or "The Quads."

Quad Cities Style Pizza: In a QC Style Pizza, brewer's malt is added to the dough, giving it a sweet, nutty taste. The dough is then hand-tossed to a quarter-inch thickness, so it's chewy when it comes out of the oven. The sauce is spicy, rather than sweet, and the fennel-spiced pork sausage goes under the cheese. Served in strips, rather than slices.

RAGBRAI: The Register's Annual Great Bike Ride Across Iowa, a weeklong tour of the state sponsored by the *Des Moines Register*. The ride is limited to 8,500 cyclists, making it the world's largest bicycle tour. The route, which varies each year, has passed through all 99 counties. Cyclists dip their wheels into the Missouri at the start of the tour and the Mississippi at the end.

Roast: Iowa raises a lot of corn and a lot of hogs, consuming both with gusto. Hog Roasts and Corn Roasts are traditional fundraisers for volunteer fire departments, politicians, schools and fraternal organizations. "Corn Roast 2015—Saturday, Aug. 22, 2 p.m. Bring a dish to pass, a meat to grill, your favorite lawn chair, any yard game you want to play, and a friend or two. We will provide plates, utensils, corn, pop, beer, wine, bottled water and grill. Cost is $4.00 which covers the beverages, corn and KYBO."—East Iowa Ski Club website.

Snake Alley: Sinuous block on North 6th Street in Burlington, with seven switchback turns in 275 feet. Designed to enable horses to climb steep Heritage Hill, Snake Alley is paved with cobblestones and rivals San Francisco's Lombard Street for crookedness. The Snake Alley Criterium is an annual bicycle race up the street.

Squinny: A chipmunk.

Tavern: A LOOSE MEAT in northwestern Iowa. Named for Ye Olde Tavern restaurant in Sioux City, which introduced the sandwich to the region.

Walk Beans: Weed a soybean field. Along with de-tasseling corn, traditional summer job for high school students.

West Coast: The Missouri River

Where Are You At?: What is your location? Midwesterners have a tendency to add "at" to this question.

MICHIGAN

30 and Out: The length of an autoworker's career, thanks to a United Auto Workers contract allowing members to retire with a full pension and benefits after three decades of service.

A-Squared: Ann Arbor. The city received its unusual name because it was, and is, well-forested, and because both its founders were married to women named Ann.

Benton Harlem: What residents of St. Joseph, the 89 percent white city on the west bank of the St. Joseph River, call Benton Harbor, the 88 percent black city on the east bank.

The Big Three: Traditionally, General Motors, Ford, and Chrysler. However, after Toyota surpassed Chrysler to become the third-best selling brand in the U.S., automotive journalists downgraded the companies to "The Detroit Three." Can also refer to Little Caesar's, Domino's, and Hungry Howie's.

Black Bottom: Detroit's original African American neighborhood, named for its fertile alluvial soil. Razed in the 1960s, as part of an urban renewal program, Black Bottom made way for the Chrysler Freeway and Lafayette Park, a modernist riverfront apartment complex designed by Mies van der Rohe. Black Bottom's residents scattered to housing projects and even more crowded slums, contributing to the tensions that caused the 1967 riot.

Blightmoor: Brightmoor, a northwest Detroit neighborhood infamous for its violence and decay.

The Bridge: The Mackinac Bridge, which spans the Straits of Mackinac, connecting the Lower Peninsula town of Mackinaw City with the Upper Peninsula town of St. Ignace. Opened November 1, 1957, just in time for deer season, which had been causing twelve-mile backups, all the way to Cheboygan, as hunters awaited ferries to take them to their U.P. camps. Pronunciation note: despite the terminal "c," it's Mack-i-NAW. Why? Because the French got their first, and that's how they spelled Michilimackinac, which they believed to be an Odawa word meaning "big turtle," a descriptor for the humped island. However, Andrew J. Blackbird, a nineteenth-century Odawa chief, insisted it was the name of the tribe that first inhabited the island. Such a symbol of Michigan that the state's food assistance card is called the Bridge Card.

Cass Corridor: The Detroit neighborhood surrounding Cass Avenue, near Wayne State University. Now that it has a Whole Foods and a Shinola watch store, it's also known as Midtown, just like the center of Manhattan.

Cereal City: Battle Creek, home of cereal giants Kellogg's and Post. A tour of the Kellogg's plant, which began by passing the Tony the Tiger statue outside the front door and ended with a sampler of tiny cereal boxes, was once an annual field trip for every southern Michigan schoolchild. When the tours ended, for reasons of safety and corporate secrecy, Kellogg's built a replica production line inside Cereal City, an amusement park designed to hawk Frosted Flakes, but that, too, is now closed.

Chevy in the Hole: An auto plant on the banks of the Flint River that ran its last shift in 1992, and was demolished a few years later. One of the sites of the 1936-37 Sit Down Strike, which led to the founding of the United Auto Workers. The plant was called Chevy in the Hole because of its low-lying location, to distinguish it from the other Chevy plants in town. Now that nothing remains but the Hole, it's being relandscaped and rebranded as Chevy Commons, a nature park sitting atop the hundred-year half-life toxins GM left behind.

Coney Island: A hot dog overlapping the edge of its bun, smothered with chili, onions, and mustard. Also known as a Coney dog. The first Coneys, as the diners that serve the dish are known, were opened by Greek and Macedonian immigrants who arrived in Detroit in the early twentieth century, after passing through New York, where they saw hot dog stands on Coney Island. A quick meal for autoworkers beginning or ending a shift, the Coney Island became Detroit's signature contribution to American fast food. The corner of Michigan Avenue and Lafayette Street is the site of Detroit's greatest culinary rivalry: American Coney Island versus Lafayette Coney Island. American was founded by brothers Bill and Gust Keros, but in 1942, a fraternal split led Bill to open Lafayette right next door. Both places serve a complete Detroit dinner: two Coney dogs, French fries, Vernors, and a slice of chocolate pie. Beyond American and Lafayette, there's the rivalry between the Detroit and Flint Coneys. The chili on the Flint Coney is packed more tightly than Detroit's runny topping.

Copper Country: The Upper Peninsula's mining region, centered on Houghton. In the nineteenth century, rich copper deposits drew immigrants from all over Europe, most numerously Cornwall and Finland. At their early twentieth-century peak, the mines yielded 266 million pounds of copper a year, but by the 1960s, they were played out. Keweenaw County, a peninsula on top of the U.P., has lost two-thirds of its population since the mining days, and now subsists on tourists who take the ferry to Isle Royale, eat thimbleberry jam from the Jampot, a bakery run by monks at the Holy Transfiguration Skete in Eagle Harbor, or drink at the Gay Bar in Gay.

The D: Nickname for Detroit. The old English D, which has been the Tigers' logo since Ty Cobb was rushing the stands to punch out a crippled fan, now represents the entire city. The *Detroit Free Press* runs photos of Detroiters displaying the D all over the world.

Devil's Night: The night before Halloween, traditionally commemorated in Detroit by setting fire to abandoned houses. In his 1990 book *Devil's Night and Other True Tales of Detroit*, Ze'ev Chafets described suburbanites dining atop the REN CEN for an aerial view of the burning city, and zipping around town with police radios to alert them to the biggest fires. Now a mostly obsolete practice since the city responded with Angels' Night, encouraging residents to patrol their neighborhoods, looking for arsonists. In 1984, there were 810 Devil's Night fires. In 2015, there were 28.

Eh: For a two-letter word, "eh" is surprisingly complex. It is not simply a punctuation signaling the end of a sentence, or an invitation to agree with the statement that follows. It's what's known as a "tag question," a conversational cue that either confirms a listener's attentiveness, or invites him to offer his own opinion or information. Suppose you're in the U.P., wearing a shirt with the name of your high school football team. If a Yooper looks at you and says, "Sexton Big Reds, eh?," what he means is "Sexton Big Reds. Never heard of them. Tell me more."
Some other examples of proper "eh" usage:
"Pretty cold today, eh?"
"Not as cold as it was last week. I had to jump my wife's car twice."
or
"I'm just gonna grab a beer, eh."
"Try the Bell's Pale Ale."
or
"Packers are looking pretty good today, eh?"
"Well, they're playing the Lions."

or

"So I'm in my tree stand, eh, and I see this six-pointer walk by."

"Yah?"

"Yah."

While so common in Canada as to be a stereotypical element of the dialect, in the United States, "eh" is used only in the U.P., northern Wisconsin, and northern Minnesota. Linguist Kathryn Remlinger theorizes that "eh" is derived from "hein," an equivalent term used by French Canadians. This would help explain its geographic distribution, since the French were the first Europeans to settle the Great Lakes. Sault Ste. Marie, Mich., the oldest city in the Midwest, was founded by the French as a fur trading post in 1667. Duluth, Minn., named for the French explorer Sieur du Lhut, has a similar history. Neither region received much English-speaking settlement until iron and copper were discovered in the nineteenth century, so the French influence endured longer there than in most parts of the Midwest.

FIP: Fucking Illinois Person, a term applied to Chicago-area vacationers who spend their summers in Southwest Michigan's HARBOR COUNTRY and drive shiny, expensive SUVs from their beachfront cottages to the ice cream stands in New Buffalo. Locals engage in the pastimes of 'FIP watching' or 'FIP hunting.'

Flintstones: A demonym for inhabitants of Flint, popularized by Mateen Cleaves, Morris Peterson, and Charlie Bell, Flint Public Schools graduates who played for Michigan State's 2000 NCAA Championship team. Replaced the older term "Flintoid," made famous by the song "I'm A Flintoid," which was sung to the tune of the Rolling Stones' "Miss You": "I work Buick all day long/ Building car doors makes me strong/ I'm a Flintoid."

Ford's: Michiganders don't shop at Kroger and K-mart, they shop at Kroger's and K-mart's. This tendency to add a possessive *s* to a business or institution dates back to the days when Henry Ford still ran his namesake car manufacturer. You didn't work at Ford, you worked at Mr. Ford's.

Freep: The *Detroit Free Press*, the state's largest newspaper.

Fudgies: Tourists who visit Mackinac Island, Traverse City, or any UP NORTH resort town with an overabundance of fudge shops. See them gawking at the fudge-making process through the window of Ryba's, on the Island. Hear them pronouncing the island's name as "Mack-in-ack." Also known as "cones," because they love gourmet ice cream, especially Moose Tracks made with Mackinac Island fudge. A year-round resident of the northern Lower Peninsula is a "permafudge."

Hamtown: Hamtramck, a formerly Polish-dominated city that now (ironically, given this nickname) has the first Muslim-majority council in the U.S.

Heikki Lunta: Fakeloric Finnish snow god created in 1970 by U.P. radio salesman David Rietta, who wrote the "Heikki Lunta Snow Dance Song" to ensure enough for a snowmobile race. It goes, in part, "We gotta have some snow by da fourth of December/ Heikki Lunta make it snow say da range club members." Heikki Lunta is a Finnish translation of Hank Snow, a then-popular country singer. At the end of winter, U.P. stations play the sequel, "Heikki Lunta Go Away." Pronounced HAY-kee LOON-ta.

Holy Wah: A YOOPER exclamation of surprise. "Holy Wah! Did you see the size of that bass?"

The Joe: Joe Louis Arena in Detroit, home of the Red Wings. Louis, who began his boxing career in Detroit, is also commemorated with a statue of his clenched hand in Hart Plaza, known simply as "The Fist."

Last Chance College: Lansing Community College, where your author began his professional writing career.

Little Missouri: A neighborhood in the Flint suburb of Burton, settled by hillbillies from the Missouri bootheel who migrated to Michigan to work in the auto plants.

Michigan Left: A traffic maneuver that involves making a right turn, then a U-turn in a dedicated lane. Thus the saying, "Right to go left." Introduced in the 1960s to relieve congestion at major intersections, Michigan Lefts are considered safer, less time-consuming, and more energy efficient that a standard left turn. The Michigan Department of Transportation claims they increase traffic capacity by up to 50 percent and reduce collisions up to 60 percent.

Michigander: Demonym for a resident of Michigan, almost universally preferred to the stilted and formal "Michiganian." The term was coined in 1848 by Whig congressman Abraham Lincoln of Illinois, as an insult to Lewis Cass, former Michigan governor and Democratic nominee for president. It combines the words "Michigan" and "gander," which then meant "silly goose" or "fool." "There is one entire article of the sort I have not discussed yet," Lincoln said. "I mean the military tail you Democrats are engaged in dovetailing onto the great Michigander."

Michissippi: Portmanteau of "Michigan" and "Mississippi," meant to reflect the slide down the demographic tables during the "Lost Decade" of the 2000s, when Michigan was the only state to lose population, and dropped to 37th in per capita income. Given the patchwork roads, the decaying cities, and the fact that half the college graduates move to Chicago as soon as they get their degrees, it is uncertain now which state this term is meant to insult.

Moo U.: Michigan State University, founded in 1855 as Michigan Agricultural College. A general term of derision applied to agricultural schools with academic pretensions. Jane Smiley's comic novel *Moo* is set at a Midwestern land grant college, inspired by her years at the University of Iowa and Iowa State.

The Motor City: Detroit. Shortened to Motown by R&B impresario Berry Gordy Jr. In the mid-1970s, when the annual death toll from the drug wars hit 714, journalists began calling Detroit "The Murder City."

Nain Rouge: A chariot-riding red demon said to appear in Detroit during moments of civic crisis—the 1805 fire, the 1967 riot. Nain Rouge has supposedly haunted Detroit ever since 1707, when the city's founder, Antoine de la Mothe Cadillac, ignored a fortune teller's advice to appease him and instead beat him with a cane. An annual Marche du Nain Rouge draws thousands of revelers who wear disguises in a campaign to drive the demon out of Detroit and lift his curse.

Paczki Day: The Polish Mardi Gras, a pre-Lenten festival in which Catholics, and other hungry people, eat paczki (pronounced PUNCH-key), which are basically bismarcks sprinkled with sugar and filled with apricot, cherry, strawberry, or chocolate. The tradition originated because Polish housewives wanted to use up their supply of sugar and lard before Lent. A paczek, as one of the pastries is called, can contain up to 700 calories. Every year, the formerly Polish-dominated city of Hamtramck holds a paczki-eating contest. The record holder consumed 23 in 15 minutes.

Party Store: A liquor store, because it sells every (legal) ingredient for a party: beer, chips, ice, stale doughnuts. "Tired of taking pop bottles back to the party store," from the Eminem song "If I Had," is the most

Michigan line in music history: it works in the fact that Michiganders call carbonated beverages "pop"; the state's ten-cent deposit law; and identifies the party store as the place to redeem the empties.

Pasty: The pasty (pronounced PAST-ee, as opposed to the tassels that swing from a burlesque dancer's breasts), is the U.P.'s signature delicacy. It was brought to the North Country by the "Cousin Jacks," Cornish miners who crossed the sea from coal to copper in the nineteenth century. Their wives, the Cousin Jennys, wanted them to carry a full meal into the mines, so they invented the pasty, a stew folded into a turnover shell. The original pasties were as complete as frozen dinners — some even had jam baked into a corner, as dessert. The miners threw away the corners, or "crimps," not only to avoid arsenic poisoning from their coal-dusted fingers, but to feed the "knockers," the ghosts living underground. A classic pasty is filled with beef, potatoes, and onions, but in America, the pasty has become as much a dumping ground of ethnic foods as the pizza. Joe's Pasty Shop in Ironwood serves the Reuben pasty, the bacon cheeseburger pasty, the taco pasty, and the Cajun chicken pasty. The Cornish pasty is the original filling, plus rutabagas.

The Ren Cen: The Renaissance Center. A septet of buildings, organized around a 73-story cylindrical tower on the Detroit riverfront. Built in the 1970s by Henry Ford II to revitalize the city's economy, it took the name of Detroit's post-riot slogan, "The Renaissance City." The promised renaissance has taken longer than the original event in Italy, but in 2004, Ford's rival, General Motors, moved its headquarters to the Ren Cen.

Ruin Porn: Photographs of blighted or abandoned buildings, devoid of any human or sociological context. Pioneered by Detroiter Lowell Boileau on his website "The Fabulous Ruins of Detroit," but most successfully exploited by photographer Andrew Moore, whose book

Detroit Disassembled included a Dali-esque image of a melted clock in a defunct school, and an empty mental health ward with the graffito "God has left Detroit." Wayne State University professor John Patrick Leary wrote that "ruin photography and ruin film aestheticizes poverty without inquiring of its origins, dramatizes spaces but never seeks out the real people who inhabit them." However, labeling a work of art or journalism "ruin porn" can also be a way to evade responsibility for Detroit's shabbiness by scolding outsiders for documenting it.

The Shop: An auto plant. An autoworker is a "shoprat."

The Soo: The area around Sault (pronounced "Soo") Ste. Marie. Sault Ste. Marie, Ontario is "Soo, Canada," while the same-named city on the American side of the St. Mary's River is "Soo, Michigan." The canal that enables ships to travel between Lake Superior and Lake Huron, bypassing the Falls of the St. Mary's, is the Soo Locks.

The Thumb: An area, shaped like the fifth digit, between Saginaw Bay and Lake St. Clair. Michiganders make much of the fact that the Lower Peninsula resembles a mitten. Ask a Michigander where she's from, and she'll flatten her right palm, then point to the spot that corresponds with her hometown's location. Traverse City is at the tip of the pinkie, Bay City in the web between thumb and forefinger, Detroit at the base of the thumb.

TOOT: Techie from Out of Town, a student at Michigan Technological University in Houghton who's not from the area, especially a TROLL who complains about the snow.

Troll: A YOOPER term for people from the Lower Peninsula, because they live under the (Mackinac) bridge. A troll who moves to the U.P. is a "Trooper."

U.P.: The Upper Peninsula, which was granted to Michigan as compensation for losing the Toledo Strip to Ohio in an 1835 boundary dispute. Most Michiganders would agree their state got the better end of that deal. YOOPERS don't call the Lower Peninsula "the L.P." They call it "downstate." The U.P. contains 30 percent of the state's landmass, but only 3 percent of the population—far less than a century ago, before the mines were emptied and the forests cut down. Now subsists on prisons and tourism, although neither is as lucrative. A U.P. politician once complained about cyclists who cross the Mackinac Bridge "with a five dollar bill and a pair of underwear, and don't change either."

Up North: Anyplace north of the Saginaw-Bay City line, but only in the Lower Peninsula. The U.P. is not "Up North." The U.P. is the U.P. Clare calls itself "Gateway to the North."

Urban Pioneer: A young, college-educated white person who moves to Detroit, reversing the white-flight migration of his parents and grandparents. The guy who refurbished a $500 house in Poletown, and got a book contract to write about the experience? Urban pioneer. Generally settle in downtown, Corktown, and Midtown— Detroit's Green Zone—making the rents in those neighborhoods more expensive than the suburbs. Detroit lost a quarter of its population in the 2000s, but the population of under-35s with college degrees increased 59 percent. Urban pioneers generally return to their suburban habitat five years after mating, when their children are ready to attend kindergarten.

Vernors: Ginger-flavored POP invented in Detroit. If you ask for ginger ale in Michigan, you may get this. Vernors with vanilla ice cream is a "Boston cooler."

Walmart Wolverine: A University of Michigan fan who has no affiliation with the school, but buys its gear at Walmart.

What up, doe?: Detroit street greeting. Originated in the 1980s among drug dealers, as a recognition of how much "dough" they were making. Title of a song by Detroit rapper Danny Brown, and used by nearly every character in the movie *8 Mile*. "What up doe can mean a few different things," a Detroiter told the website allhiphop.com. "It can be a greeting, a challenge, or a phrase used to determine one's origin or residency…It depends on the situation and voice inflection. Whenever a Detroiter hears that, wherever they may be, they know home isn't that far away."

Windsor Ballet: Strip clubs in Windsor, Ontario, on the other side of the Detroit River, directly south of Detroit, featuring French Canadian dancers from Montreal. Ontario allows nudie bars to serve liquor, while Michigan does not. There is actually a legitimate Windsor Ballet, which does not appreciate the comparison.

Yoopers: In 1979, the *Escanaba Daily Press* held a contest to name the inhabitants of the U.P. "Yooper" was the winning entry. Fond of snowmobiling in the winter, all-terrain vehicles in the summer, deer hunting in the fall, snowshoeing in the spring (at least until the snow melts in May), and beer drinking year round. Speak a dialect known as "Yoopanese," which features Canadian raising, the use of "eh" as a conversational cue, and "youse" as a second-person plural. Some Yoopanese terms include "chook" for hat, "mitts" for gloves, "swampers" for rubber-soled boots, "pank" for patting-down snow, and "snow cow" for fat girl. You can spot a Yooper by the "Say Yah to Da U.P., Eh!" bumper sticker on his truck. The comic band Da Yoopers is best known for their song "Second Week of Deer Camp."

Ypsiltucky: Ypsilanti, one of several auto-making towns overrun by Southerners who migrated to Michigan to work in THE SHOP. Now getting a reputation as Ann Arbor's Brooklyn, a creative class ghetto for artists who are drawn to the university town's culture, but can't afford its rent.

Yup: An indication of agreement, pronounced "Yuhhhp." The Northern Cities Vowel Shift causes Inland North speakers to make short *e*'s sound like *u*'s. For example, "seven" becomes "suvun." "You're from Ionia? Don't they have a free fair there every summer?" "Yuhhhp."

MINNESOTA

Alex: Nickname for Alexandria. Pronounce it "Alek," or you'll sound like a CITIOT.

Alexander: Brandy Alexander. Minnesota drinks more brandy per capita than any state.

APHC: *A Prairie Home Companion*, a public radio program founded by Garrison Keillor, first broadcast from St. Paul in 1974. A revival of old-timey radio variety hours, the show features folk music and comic skits about such sacred Upper Midwestern institutions as deer hunting and Lutheranism. Its signature monologue is the weekly "News from Lake Wobegon," a fictional small town based on Stearns County, where Keillor lived as a struggling young writer. Keillor retired in 2016 but the show, though still based in St. Paul, has become a nationwide phenomenon: broadcast on 400 stations, on the cover of *Time* magazine, performed in amphitheaters coast to coast, adapted for the big screen. All of which is quite un-Minnesotan.

The Arrowhead: The northeastern corner of the state, starting in Duluth, because it is shaped like the tip of an arrow aimed at Lake Superior. The Lake Superior coastline, which includes the taconite ports of Two Harbors and Silver Bay, and the art gallery/fishing village of Grand Marais, is known as the North Shore.

Baja Minnesota: Dismissive term for Iowa.

Barnelopet: A cross-country ski race for children, sponsored by a Sons of Norway lodge.

Bars: Pastries served in an 8"x13" baking dish and cut up into rectangular portions. Rice Krispie treats topped with butterscotch and chocolate—known as Scotcheroos—are a classic example of bars. Bars are set at the end of the potluck table, as dessert after HOTDISH.

Boiled Dinner: A one-pot dish of beef, onions, potatoes, and carrots, simmered for hours in broth. In most places, cooked only on St. Patrick's Day, but available year-round in some IRON RANGE restaurants.

Breezers: Hockey pants.

Cake Eater: A resident of Edina, a wealthy Twin Cities suburb whose name is said to be an acronym for "Every Day I Need Attention." From "Let them eat cake," Marie Antoinette's dismissal of the poor. In the Minnesota-set youth hockey movie *The Mighty Ducks*, a member of the scrappy team from the wrong side of the tracks calls a member of the rich, snobby team a cake eater.

The Chimney: Colloquial name for the Northwest Angle, the only part of the continental United States north of the 49th parallel, because its border forms a rectangle sticking out above the rest of the state. This cartographic oddity occurred because the Treaty of Paris, which ended the American Revolution, specified that the border between the U.S. and British Canada was to proceed to the northwest corner of Lake of the Woods, then due west to the headwaters of the Mississippi. The negotiators didn't realize that Lake Itasca, the source of the Mississippi, is south of Lake of the Woods. To correct for the error, surveyors drew a borderline from the lake to the 49th parallel, isolating a 123-square mile peninsula inside the United States. The village of Angle Inlet is a busy fishing resort, but anglers have to drive through Canada to get there.

The Cities: Minneapolis and St. Paul, the state's two largest cities, which sit side by side along the Mississippi River. The term "Twin Cities" (which inspired the Minnesota Twins' name) is rarely used by Minnesotans, who also call them "The Metro" or "The Metro Area." The Cities aren't exactly twins, either: Minneapolis is cosmopolitan and Protestant, St. Paul staid and Catholic.

Citiot: A tourist from THE CITIES who visits northern Minnesota. Also known as "612er," after The Cities' area code.

DFL: The Democratic-Farmer-Labor Party, a political agglomeration unique to Minnesota. The DFL was founded in 1944, when Minneapolis Mayor Hubert Humphrey engineered a merger between his Democrats and the populist Farmer-Labor Party. Besides Humphrey, famous DFLers include Eugene McCarthy, Walter Mondale, Paul Wellstone, and Al Franken. The party has been enormously successful in Minnesota, which has voted DFL in every presidential elections since 1976—the longest current streak in the nation. Minnesotans like to brag that theirs is the only state never to vote for Ronald Reagan.

Dry: A changing room for iron miners, where they hang wet clothes in baskets after a sweaty shift underground.

Fish House: A fishing shanty dragged out onto a lake every winter. Built of plywood, includes holes for fishing lines, old chairs for sitting and waiting for a strike, hooks for coats and tackle, a propane heater, and an auger for drilling through the ice. A four-by-eight has two holes in the floor, an eight-by-eight has four. In the movie *Grumpy Old Men*, Old Man Gustafson's fish house is outfitted with a TV for watching hockey.

Homer Hanky: A white handkerchief with an image of a red baseball, produced by the *Star Tribune* newspaper during the Twins' 1987 playoff run, which culminated in a World Series victory. Fans waved the hankies during games at the since-demolished Hubert H. Humphrey Metrodome (known as The Dome or the HomerDome). Now a Twins tradition, new Homer Hankies are produced every time the team makes the playoffs.

Hotdish: A casserole served in a baking dish, usually containing ground beef, green beans, and cream of mushroom soup, and sometimes topped with tater tots. Minnesotans also refer to Hungarian goulash as "hotdish." Indispensable at potlucks and church suppers. The Minnesota congressional delegation competes in an annual hotdish competition, founded in 2010 by Sen. Al Franken.

Iron Range: The mining region of northeastern Minnesota, including Virginia, Hibbing, and Eveleth. Produces taconite that is shipped to the steel mills of the lower Great Lakes. Also known as "The Range," pronounced locally as "Da Raynch." Inhabitants are "Iron Rangers" or "Rangers."

Jeet?: Have you had your SUPPER yet?

Jucy Lucy: A hamburger with a pool of melted cheese in the middle. Matt's Bar and Grill and the 5-8 Club in Minneapolis have a longstanding dispute over which establishment invented the burger, and even how it's spelled. According to Matt's website, "the "Jucy Lucy" was created when a local customer asked for two hamburger patties with a slice of cheese in the middle. Upon biting into this new, molten hot burger, he exclaimed "that's one juicy Lucy," and a legend was born: "Customer demand grew so quickly, we forgot to add the *i*." The 5-8 Club spells the meal "Juicy Lucy," and waitstaff wear shirts declaring "If It's Spelled Right, It's Done Right."

"Let It Curl!": Curling term meaning "Don't sweep; let the rock slide." As further proof it is the most Canadian state in the union, Minnesota has a vibrant curling scene, inspired by a 2006 Olympic bronze medal won by a team from Bemidji.

Little Brown Jug: The oldest traveling trophy in big-time college football, awarded to the winner of the Minnesota-Michigan game. According to the University of Minnesota athletic department, Michigan coach Fielding H. Yost left behind an earthenware jug after a 1903 tie in Minneapolis. He wrote to ask for it back, and received this reply: "If you want it, you'll have to win it." Michigan has, over and over again, leading the series 70-23-3.

Lutefisk: A traditional Norwegian fish recipe eaten around Christmastime. Lutefisk is dried cod soaked in lye, which gives it a spongy texture. Rather flavorless as a result, the fish is served with white sauce and alongside lefse, a potato flatbread. A holiday staple at church suppers and VFW fundraisers, lutefisk is an important element of Scandinavian-American identity, much more widely consumed in the Upper Midwest than in Norway or Sweden.

The 'Mats: The Replacements, 1980s Minneapolis post-punk band renowned for their drunken performances, and for inspiring the sounds of grunge and alt rock. Nicknamed "The Placemats" by a hater, the band sportingly shortened it to The 'Mats.

Minnesota Nice: An attitude of agreeableness, politeness, communitarianism, and aversion to conflict, inherited from reserved, socialistic Scandinavians who settled the state. Minnesota Nice is cited as a source of the state's liberal politics, its high level of support for public radio, and its low levels of crime and violence. However, outsiders complain that Minnesotans are so intent on minding their own business and so reluctant to express their feelings that they're impossible to get to know.

Mojakka: A soup with beef, carrots, onions, celery and potatoes. It's also known as "Finnish soup," but the word comes from the Serbo-Croatian *mojo yuka*, which means "my soup." In the ethnic mixing of the northern Minnesota iron mines, Finns adopted the recipe and gave it a Finnish-style spelling, even though the soup in unknown in Finland.

MPR: Minnesota Public Radio. Although the first public radio station was in Madison, Wis., Minnesota produced the medium's first superstar—*A Prairie Home Companion*'s Garrison Keillor—and established its Upper Midwestern aesthetic: soft-spoken, non-confrontational, and as inoffensive as a Methodist sermon. MPR's founding station, KSJR at St. John's University in St. Cloud, also participated in founding National Public Radio in the early 1970s.

Nodaker: A North Dakotan.

Nordeast: Northeast Minneapolis, which was originally settled by Scandinavians.

Oh Fer: An intensifier, most commonly used by women, as a prefix to the quality being described. "Here's a picture of our daughter." "Oh, fer cute!" "Ma, you forgot to turn left there." "Oh, fer dumb!"

Oh, Sure: An acknowledgement of agreement. Less emphatic than YOU BET.

Ole and Lena: Proverbial husband and wife in "dumb Norskie" jokes aimed at Scandinavian immigrants (and later told by their children and grandchildren). Example: Ole and Lena were driving to Minneapolis on their honeymoon. Ole put his hand on Lena's knee. "You can go farder if you vant," Lena giggled. So Ole drove to Duluth.

On/Off Sale: A tavern which also sells beer and liquor to go.

Rachel: A reuben sandwich made with turkey, instead of corned beef.

Scandifarian: A white person with dreadlocks, usually blond. The most famous example is Dave Pirner, singer and guitarist for the Minneapolis band Soul Asylum, who sported dreads during his early '90s commercial peak.

Scandihoovian: Originally a disparaging term for Swedish and Norwegian immigrants. Now used proudly by Minnesotans of Scandinavian descent.

Skol, Vikings!: Minnesota Vikings cheer, taken from a Scandinavian toast. The Vikings were named in honor of the state's Scandinavian population, and the Kensington runestone, supposedly left behind by Vikings who visited the state in 1362.

The State of Hockey: Anthem of the Minnesota Wild, the state's second NHL franchise. (The first, the Minnesota North Stars, moved to Dallas in 1993.) Despite its lack of professional success, Minnesota is the nation's most hockey-mad state, with more youth players (54,000) and more NHL players all time (247) than any other. The Boy's High School Hockey Tournament not only draws bigger crowds to the Xcel Center than the Wild, it's the best-attended high school sports championship in the country. Herb Brooks, coach of the 1980 U.S. Olympic hockey team, was a Minnesotan, and has a rink named after him at St. Cloud State University—one of five Division I hockey schools in the state.

Strib: The *Star Tribune*, Minneapolis's daily newspaper.

Supper: There are three meals a day in Minnesota: breakfast, dinner, and supper. Lunch is a snack squeezed in between breakfast and dinner or dinner and supper.

Uff Da: An exclamation of exasperation, often uttered after a surprising event. "Uff da, look at da dent I put in my car." Or "Uff da, dat's a lotta snow to shovel." The Scandinavian equivalent of the Jewish "oy vey" or the Spanish "ay caramba." It is allegedly of Norwegian origin, but is seldom heard in Norway.

The X: Xcel Energy Center, concert arena and home of the Minnesota Wild.

Yah: All-purpose affirmative, likely derived from the German *ja*. "Ya got plans this weekend?" "Yah, we're goin' down to the Cities to see the Wolves play."
or
"Seen your new truck. She runnin' good?" "Oh, yah, she's runnin' great."

You Bet/You Betcha: An enthusiastic term of agreement. "Hey, is it OK if I try out your rod and reel?" "You bet!"
or
"I need to step away for a minute and use the restroom." "You bet!" "You bet" is much more common than "you betcha," which is usually used ironically, by speakers trying to exaggerate their Minnesota-ness. "I hear you serve good lutefisk here." "You betcha!" On *APHC*, a guest told a joke about a Palestinian woman and a Minnesota man who named their son "Yassir Youbetcha."

OHIO

"Ann Arbor is a Whore": Ohio State taunt to "That School Up North"—the University of Michigan, its historical football rival. Buckeye fans also like to sing, "We don't give a damn about the whole state of Michigan, we're from O-hi-o!"

Battle of Ohio: The rivalry between the Cleveland Browns and the Cincinnati Bengals, which began after the Bengals joined the NFL in 1968. So caustic is the enmity between the two teams (and the two cities) that when Bengals fans threw garbage on the field during a game against the Seahawks, Coach Sam Wyche got on the PA to remind them, "You don't live in Cleveland, you live in Cincinnati."

The Best Damn Band in the Land: The Ohio State University marching band, known for forming intricate shapes—a *T. Rex*, Superman lifting a falling building—and for playing "Hang On, Sloopy," the official state rock song.

Black Monday: Monday, September 19, 1977, the day Youngstown Sheet & Tube announced it would shut down its Campbell Works, which employed 5,000 steelworkers. Occurring amidst a nationwide steel crisis, it was the beginning of the end of Youngstown's prosperity. In the next few years, U.S. Steel and Republic Steel abandoned Youngstown; the city eventually lost half its population.

Brier Hill: A Youngstown style of pizza with red sauce, red and green peppers, and Romano cheese, named for the neighborhood that contained the city's Little Italy. Most Youngstown pizzerias serve a Brier Hill; St. Anthony's Church (in Brier Hill) makes them every Friday.

Buckeyes: Chocolate-covered peanut butter balls, designed to look like the brown-and-beige nut of Ohio's state tree.

City Chicken: Pork cubes served on skewers. During the Depression, and before the era of factory farming, chicken was an expensive delicacy (hence President Hoover's promise of "a chicken in every pot"). Hard-pressed urban housewives bought pork instead, sometimes shaping it into drumsticks to fool their families.

Cleveland-style Polka: Musical genre popularized by Cleveland-born, Slovenian-America accordionist Frankie Yankovic, polka's biggest star during its 1940s and '50s heyday. Slovenian polkas, which are slower than the Polish and German variations, are descended from the Viennese waltzes once popular throughout the Austro-Hungarian Empire. The National Cleveland-Style Polka Hall of Fame and Museum in North Euclid memorializes the songs put out of style by the music in the Rock and Roll Hall of Fame.

Cookie Table: At Youngstown wedding receptions, there is always a dessert table with plates of kolacky, pizzele, baklava, and other Old World pastries. The custom originated during the Depression, when intermarriages between ethnic groups were common, and no one could afford a wedding cake.

Crooked River: The Cuyahoga River, which is crumpled into so many kinks and loops as it approaches Lake Erie that the water takes a week to flow the final five miles. Contrary to local belief, the name actually means "big river" in Mohawk. Crooked River Brewing Co., Crooked River Skate Park, and Cleveland author Mark Winegardner's novel *Crooked River Burning* all take their names from the Cuyahoga.

Dawg Pound: The Cleveland Browns cheering section in the east end zone of FirstEnergy Stadium. The Dawg Pound originated in the old Municipal Stadium (the Muny) in the 1980s, after cornerback Hanford Dixon nicknamed the defense "Dogs," because they chased cat-like quarterbacks. Fans threw Milk Bone dog biscuits, batteries, snowballs, and turkey legs at opposing players. The new Dawg Pound is considerably more expensive and less rowdy than the Muny's.

Devil Strip: Akron term for the grassy area between the sidewalk and the street. Said to have been invented by West Virginians who migrated to work in the city's rubber factories, as a way of warning their newly urbanized children not to get too close to the street. In Cleveland, it's called a "tree lawn," even though it's more common to see a garbage can than a tree there.

Ditch: To cut in line, in the Columbus area.

Dolly Parton Towers: Procter & Gamble headquarters in downtown Cincinnati, because the twin buildings resemble giant pointed breasts. Also known as "The Soap Factory."

Ethnic: A Northeast Ohioan of Central or Eastern European descent. After the Austro-Hungarian Empire broke up, it reassembled in Cleveland. A young disc jockey who didn't want to admit to playing polka told girls it was "ethnic jazz."

Factory of Sadness: FirstEnergy Stadium, home of the Cleveland Browns. Filled with fans who hate Cleveland, the Browns, and themselves, for living in Cleveland and rooting for the Browns. Ask Siri to locate "sadness," and it directs you here.

Goetta: A sausage patty composed of pork and/or beef, steel-cut oats, onions, and spices, brought to Cincinnati by German immigrants. Pronounced "GETT-uh."

The Ice Castle: Youngstown State University's Stambaugh Stadium, where the Penguins play football.

"I'm going over the river": A Cincinnatian is going to Kentucky

The Jake: Progressive Field, home of the Cleveland Indians. Despite the corporate re-naming, the stadium is still known by the diminutive of Jacobs Field, as it was called from its construction by Indians owner Richard Jacobs in 1994 until 2008, when Progressive Insurance paid $57.6 million for the rights. Sold out 455 consecutive home games from 1995 to 2001, as the Indians looked like they were about to win their first World Series since 1948. They didn't, losing to the Braves in 1995 and the Marlins in 1997.

Jeezle Pete!: Jeez o' Pete, to a Cincinnatian.

Jenny: The Jeannette Blast Furnace at the Brier Hill Plant of the Youngstown Sheet & Tube Co. Following the convention of naming blast furnaces after women, its namesake was Mary Jeanette Thomas, daughter of the company president. After YS&T shut down, Jenny became a symbol of Youngstown's steel-making past. Bruce Springsteen referred to it in his song "Youngstown," and local historians attempted to turn it into a museum. Their efforts failed, and Jenny was demolished in 1997.

The Mistake on the Lake: Derogatory nickname for Cleveland, referencing the city's location on Lake Erie, and its streak of hard luck from the late 1960s to the late 1970s, beginning with the

Cuyahoga River fire and ending with the first municipal bankruptcy since the Great Depression under Mayor Dennis Kucinich. Also referred to Municipal Stadium, whose 74,000 seats the perennially losing Browns and Indians were unable to fill.

The 'Nati: Nickname for Cincinnati. Also known as Cincy and the Queen City, because it was once the nation's largest inland city, referred to as "Queen of the West" in Henry Wadsworth Longfellow's 1854 poem "Catawba Wine." The nickname City of Seven Hills referred to ridges overlooking the Ohio River, and was meant to encourage an association with Rome.

"The Neighborhood Has Changed": A Clevelander's (more likely, a Cleveland suburbanite's) euphemistic way of explaining she left her old neighborhood because it was colonized by "the element."

OTR: Over-the-Rhine, a historic neighborhood in Cincinnati. Originally populated by German immigrants, who named the Miami and Erie Canal after the river back home. Declined to dereliction in the twentieth century, reaching a nadir with a 2001 race riot over the police shooting of an unarmed black man. That drove down property values enough to attract hipster record and T-shirt shops to OTR's Italianate rowhouses; it is now one of the city's least affordable neighborhoods.

Party Plates: Red-on-yellow license plates issued to motorists convicted of Driving Under the Influence. Also known as "scarlet letter" plates.

Please?: "Pardon" or "I didn't understand you" in Cincinnati. A remnant of the city's German heritage: a German who misunderstands a speaker says *bitte*, or "please." "May I mamo dogface to the banana patch?" "Please?"

Polish Boy: Cleveland's hometown sandwich: kielbasa with cole slaw and French fries, smothered in barbecue sauce.

Porkopolis: Cincinnati, because its German immigrants raised and slaughtered so many pigs. The first salt pork plant opened in 1818, shipping its products down the Ohio and Mississippi rivers. Procter & Gamble rendered pig fat into soap. During the Civil War, Cincinnati lost its role as the nation's slaughterhouse to Chicago, which could ship pork to troops by rail, bypassing the Confederate-held Mississippi. This ended Cincinnati's bid to become the Midwest's pre-eminent city, and led to the WINDY CITY insult. The city's meatpacking roots are still celebrated with the Flying Pig Marathon and a winged metal pig above a bridge to Kentucky. The slaughterhouses also inspired the song "The Cincinnati Dancing Pig."

Proctoid: An employee of Cincinnati-based Procter & Gamble.

The Q: Quicken Loans Arena, home of the Cleveland Cavaliers, which are owned by Rust Belt sugar daddy Dan Gilbert, founder of Quicken Loans.

Rust Belt: Toward the end of his hopeless campaign against Ronald Reagan in 1984, Walter Mondale told steelworkers at the LTV mill in Cleveland that "Mr. Reagan's policy toward the industrial belt of America is 'let it rust,'" and that he was turning the Midwest into "a rust bowl." The phrase was meant to evoke the Dust Bowl of the Great Depression. While Mondale introduced the term to political discourse, it had been used in a 1982 *Time* magazine article titled "Booms, Busts and the Birth of a Rust Bowl." Rust Bowl soon underwent a journalistic transformation to Rust Belt, so it conformed to other regional labels such as Bible Belt and Sun Belt, and became the post industrial replacement for "The Arsenal of Democracy."

Sauerkraut Balls: Sauerkraut, sausage, onions, cream cheese, and egg, all rolled into a tiny globe of Northeast Ohio gluttony. The recipe sounds Slavic, but sauerkraut balls were invented in Akron, as an *hors d'oeuvre*.

The Schott: Shorter name for the Value City Arena at the Jerome Schottenstein Center, home of Ohio State basketball.

The Shoe: Ohio State's football stadium, which is shaped like a giant horseshoe.

Three-Way: Spaghetti covered with chili and shredded cheese. A four-way adds onions or beans. A five-way adds onions *and* beans. Best eaten at Skyline Chili in Cincinnati. Before the chili is served, the server sets out a bowl of oyster crackers. Customers poke holes in the crackers and dribble in hot sauce to make "Cracker Bombs."

"Where did you go to school?": A proper question to ask a stranger in Cincinnati. Cincinnati has a high percentage of natives living within its borders, which has in turn resulted in an insular culture, as well as a strong Catholic heritage, which has resulted in a large parochial school attendance. "Where did you go to school?" is understood as a question about high school. The answer reveals whether the person is a Cincinnatian (and from which neighborhood), a Catholic, how wealthy, and how academically oriented.

Who Dey?: Call and response cheer of Cincinnati Bengals fans. "Who dey, who dey, who dey think gonna beat dem Bengals?" "Nobody." One theory holds that it originated from beer vendors shouting "Hudy!," short for Hudepohl, Cincinnati's hometown lager.

The Yo: Youngstown, also known as Y-Town or Murder City.

You Screwed Up: Youngstown State University. If you hadn't, you'd be at Ohio State.

Youngstown Tune-up: A car bomb. Too small to have its own mob, Youngstown was the site of turf wars between the Cleveland and Pittsburgh mobs. Blowing up a rival's car was a favorite method of assassination.

PITTSBURGH

Arn City: Iron City beer, a hometown lager first brewed in Pittsburgh in 1861. Also called "I.C.," or "Arn Shitty." A shot of Imperial whiskey with an Iron City is an "Imp 'n' Arn."

Black and Gold: The colors of all three professional sports teams: the Pirates, the Steelers, and the Penguins. Almost every Pittsburgher has at least one black and gold garment, and more likely ten. TV news broadcasters are expected to dress in the civic colors on Steeler Sundays.

The Buccos: The Pirates (who adopted their nickname after being accused of stealing players from other teams). Short for "Buccaneers."

The Burgh: Nickname for Pittsburgh.

Carline: Streetcar track.

Chipped Chopped ham: A marbled loaf formed of mashed-together ham chunks. A specialty of Isaly's, which sells it at supermarket deli counters and serves it sliced thinly in HOAGIES at its few remaining take-out restaurants.

Dahntahn: Downtown.

The Frick: A museum complex on the estate of nineteenth-century steel magnate Henry Clay Frick. Includes an auto collection, an art gallery, and Frick's mansion.

The Golden Triangle: DAHNTAHN Pittsburgh, where it narrows toward THE POINT at which the Monongahela and Allegheny rivers flow together.

Gumband: A rubber band. A Pittsburgher who moves away then returns home is a "gumbander," because he rebounded to his native city.

The Hill: The Hill District, Pittsburgh's original African-American neighborhood. The setting for many of the plays of August Wilson, a Hill native.

Hoagie: A submarine sandwich.

Hunky: A derogatory term for Czech, Slovak, Croatian, and Hungarian immigrants, and their supposedly uncouth behavior. Both a noun and an adjective. "You didn't set the table right. Don't be Hunky." "That babushka makes you look Hunky."

Jag: A Scots-Irish word meaning thorn, or to be pricked. "Be careful of the jags on that rose. Don't jag yourself."

Jagoff: An irritating or obnoxious person. "Hey, jagoff! Choose a lane!" "That jagoff was supposed to fix the furnace today, but he didn't show up." From the word JAG, meaning to prick. "Quit jaggin' around" means "quit fooling around." In 2012, *Pittsburgh Post-Gazette* editor David Shribman—a Massachusetts native—attracted local ridicule when he banned "jagoff" from his newspaper, despite being fully aware of its non-obscene provenance.

Jumbo: A fried bologna sandwich.

Kennywood's open: Your fly's unzipped. A reference to Kennywood, a local amusement park. At the fast-food restaurant Eat'n Park, a sign inside the men's room asks departing urinators, "Is Kennywood Open?"

Mon Valley: The Monongahela Valley, named after the river that joins the Allegheny in Pittsburgh to form the Ohio. The valley lies south of the city, and was once an active steel-making area. The Homestead Works, which was the world's largest mill before its closure in 1986, was built on the banks of the Mon.

N'at: Et cetera. "Paul's gonna set up the tree stand and get the decorations n'at." It is assumed that listeners will know what else Paul is going to, and don't need to be bothered or patronized with the details.

Nebby: Nosy. A nosy person is a "nebshit."

North Hills and South Hills: Suburbs of Pittsburgh, divided by the rivers. North Hills residents never go to South Hills, and vice versa, although both will go DAHNTAHN. As the saying goes, "You don't cross THE POINT."

The "O": The basic offering of The Original Hot Dog Shop, which opened next to Forbes Field in 1960, and survived the ballpark's demise.

Philthadelphia Flyers: The Philadelphia Flyers, the Penguins' cross-state rivals.

Pittsburgh Toilet: When Pittsburgh was a steelmaking town, men came home from the mills covered in soot. Their wives didn't want them tracking that filth through the house, so they installed a toilet and sink in the basement, where the husbands could clean up before heading upstairs. The most elaborate basements also include a Pittsburgh shower, an unenclosed nozzle over a drain.

The Point: Where the Allegheny and the Monongahela meet to form the Ohio. Once the site of French Fort Duquesne, which was captured by the British during the French and Indian War, and renamed Fort Pitt, in honor of British politician and civic namesake William Pitt, First Earl of Chatham.

Primanti Sandwich: A sandwich with cole slaw, tomato, French fries, and your choice of meat between slices of Italian bread. (A hamburger patty is most popular, but pastrami is the best.) Served at Primanti Bros., the eponymous restaurant. Pittsburghers love to put French fries on salads and sandwiches.

"Raise the Jolly Roger": During Pirates rallies, fans are encouraged to cheer on the team by waving skull and crossbones flags.

Redd Up: Clean up. "Redd up your room! We're having company." When PNC Park hosted the All-Star Game in 2006, the city launched a "Redd Up Pittsburgh" campaign to make the town spiffy for tourists.

"Scratch my back with a hacksaw!": One of the many inscrutable goal calls of Penguins announcers Mike Lange. Others include "Let's go hunt moose on a Harley," "He's smiling like a butcher's dog," "Call Arnold Slick from Turtle Crick!" and "He doesn't know whether to cry or wind his watch." Collectively, these sayings are known as "Lange-isms."

Sliberty: East Liberty Boulevard.

Slippy: Slippery

Steel City: Pittsburgh's traditional name for itself. Although steel is no longer produced in the city, it paid for most of the universities, churches, and mansions.

Sweeper: Vacuum cleaner.

Steeler Nation: The Steelers' following, which reaches far beyond Pittsburgh, because the team was at its' peak in the 1970s, when football became a widely viewed TV sport, and because so many Pittsburghers left home to look for work during and after the 1980s steel crisis.

The Strip: The Strip District, a stretch of Penn Avenue between 16th and 24th streets, known especially for produce wholesalers and souvenir shops.

The Terrible Towel: A gold-colored rally towel introduced in 1975 by Steelers broadcaster and all-around Yinzer Myron Cope. Fans were encouraged to cheer on the Steelers by twirling the towel over their heads. That season, the team won the second of its six Super Bowls, against the Dallas Cowboys.

Tube: A tunnel through one of Pittsburgh's hills. The Liberty Tubes take cars through Mt. Washington.

The Warhol: The Andy Warhol Museum, the largest museum in the United States devoted to a single artist. Warhol grew up in Pittsburgh, studying commercial art at the Carnegie Institute of Technology before moving to New York.

Yinz: The second person plural of "you," and the definitive Pittsburgh word. "Are yinz goin' dahntahn to watch the Stillers game?" A shortening of the Scots-Irish "you uns," yinz is unique to western Pennsylvania, and is so associated with the region that heavily-accented locals are known as "Yinzers."

The Yock: The Youghiogheny (pronounced YOCK-a-gainy) River, a tributary of the Mon.

ST. LOUIS

AB: Anheuser Busch, brewers of Budweiser. Founded in St. Louis in 1852, sold to the Belgian conglomerate InBev in 2008.

The Arch: The Gateway Arch, a parabolic monument on the Mississippi River erected in 1965 to commemorate St. Louis's role as a jumping-off point for Western exploration. Officially known as the Jefferson National Expansion Memorial, it symbolizes St. Louis the way the Eiffel Tower symbolizes Paris. St. Louis is often called "Arch City."

Brain Sandwich: Fried calves' brains on rye bread. Widely enjoyed when St. Louis was a slaughterhouse town, now served in only a few south St. Louis taverns, which switched to pigs' brains after the Mad Cow scare.

The Brewery: The Anheuser-Busch brewery, which scents the air of the nearby Soulard neighborhood with malt and hops.

Burnt Ends: Chunks of meat from the fatty tip of a brisket. A staple of St. Louis-style barbecue, in which the meat is dry rubbed and diners are given a choice of sauces (usually sweet and tomato based) to apply after grilling. Local barbecue features pork steak—the shoulder of a pig—and the St. Louis-style rib rack, which is squared off by sawing away the tips. St. Louisans also eat pig snoots grilled to a crisp.

Catty Corner: Diagonally across the street.

Concrete: Soft ice cream so thick it clings to a cup when turned upside down. First served in 1959 at Ted Drewes Frozen Custard, which still attracts long lines of ice cream fans.

Corkball: A street game played with a long, thin bat and a miniature baseball.

The County: St. Louis County, which surrounds the city proper on three sides. As an independent city, St. Louis is not part of the county. South County, Mid County, and West County are genteel, white, and suburban. North County, or NoCo, is a destination for African-Americans from the North Side of St. Louis; it contains Ferguson, which became world famous as the site of protests over the police shooting of Michael Brown, an unarmed black youth.

The Depressed Section: A stretch of I-70 in downtown St. Louis that runs below street grade. The city built a park over the highway, to make the view less depressing.

Derrty: Your best friend, your homeboy. At the beginning of his "Right Thurr" video, Chingy can be heard calling "Hey, Derrty" to an offscreen figure. Nelly's record label is called Derrty Entertainment. If you're old school, your best friend is your "mo."

The East Side: East St. Louis and other seamy trans-Mississippi suburbs in Illinois. Going to the East Side for a night of strip clubs, gambling, and massages with happy endings is called "Doin' the East Side Boogie."

Farty: Forty. "There's a wreck on HIGHWAY FARTY." St. Louis often substitute an *a* sound for *o*'s following consonants. "Good marning" is an a.m. greeting.

Frozen Fishbowl: A 32-ounce frozen glass goblet of beer at Rigazzi's, an Italian restaurant in THE HILL.

Gooey Butter Cake: A pastry invented in St. Louis when a baker used sticky butter instead of smooth in a coffee cake. The bakery cut up the resulting concoction into bars, and it became a local hit. Warning: the recipe calls for half a cup of butter and an eight-ounce package of cream cheese.

Halloween Jokes: On Halloween, St. Louis children are expected to tell jokes before receiving their candy. An example: "Why do witches wear name tags? To tell which witch is which."

Hands Up, Don't Shoot: Slogan that originated during the protests against the 2014 fatal police shooting of unarmed black teenager Michael Brown in the NORTH COUNTY suburb of Ferguson, based on stories that Brown raised his hands before police fired. Simply raising hands became a gesture of solidarity, employed by members of the St. Louis Rams and the Congressional Black Caucus.

Highway 40: U.S. Route 40, the so-called National Road, was a two-lane highway that ran from Atlantic City to San Francisco. When the stretch that passed through St. Louis was replaced with Interstate 64, St. Louisans refused to give up the old name. Signs for I-64 and U.S. 40 appear on the highway, and locals refer to it as "Highway Farty."

The Hill: An Italian-American neighborhood known for its trattorias, bakeries, bocce courts, St. Ambrose Catholic Church, and fire hydrants painted red, white, and green. Major league catchers Yogi Berra and Joe Garagiola grew up across the street from each other in the Hill.

Hoosier: A low-class, uncultured person. Adopted by St. Louisans as a term of derision after Indiana natives came to work in a Chrysler plant in Fenton in the 1960s and 1970s, bringing their country ways; now applied to all rednecks. "They still have their Christmas lights up in February; that's so Hoosier." The word has become so ingrained in the St. Louis lexicon it has taken on multiple meanings. White trash with money is the "Hoosiosie." If a Hoosier puts on airs by moving to the wealthy suburb of Ladue, he becomes a "Ladoosier." A working class Jew is a "Jewsier."

Hurr and Thurr: Black St. Louisans stretch out the *r* sound at the end of words. They also use *er* at the beginning of words, so "everywhere" sounds like "airr-wairr." Nelly's "Hot in Herre" and Chingy's "Right Thurr" both employ this linguistic feature.

I-70 Series: Originally the 1985 World Series between the Cardinals and the Kansas City Royals, after the highway that runs between the two cities. Now the annual interleague series between the teams.

The Landing: Laclede's Landing, a riverfront dining and entertainment district on the spot where Pierre Laclede founded St. Louis in 1764, so the French could get away from the English after losing their colonies east of the Mississippi. In the Wilco song "Heavy Metal Drummer," Belleville, Illinois, native Jeff Tweedy sings of seeing heavy metal bands "on the Landing in the summer." That's a reference to the now-closed nightclub Mississippi Nights.

The Loop: The Delmar Loop, the stretch of Delmar Boulevard straddling St. Louis and U CITY where streetcars turned around. Now the site of the St. Louis Walk of Fame and the nightclub Blueberry Hill, where St. Louis Walk of Famer and Rock and Roll Hall of Famer Chuck Berry played a monthly show for nearly 20 years.

The Lou: Nickname for St. Louis. Popularized by local rapper Nelly in his song "Country Grammar": "Sing it loud/I'm from the Lou and I'm proud."

The Man: Cardinals Hall of Fame first baseman Stan Musial, namesake of the Stan Musial Veterans Memorial Bridge. The bridge connects Missouri and Illinois, and is known as "The Stan Span."

Missour-ee vs. Missour-ah: Competing pronunciations of the state's name. Generally, Missour-ah is associated with older, rural residents, and is losing ground to Missour-ee, which is preferred in St. Louis, as well as Kansas City and Columbia, home of the University of Missouri. Former U.S. Attorney General John Ashcroft, who grew up in Springfield, says "Missour-ah," but many politicians use both pronunciations, depending on where they're campaigning. Sen. Claire McCaskill recorded advertisements with "Missour-ee" for urban stations and "Missour-ah" for rural stations.

Mizzou: The University of Missouri at Columbia. Its cheer is "Mizzou-rah!"

Old Cathedral: The Basilica of St. Louis, King, which represents the first Catholic parish in St. Louis, founded by Pierre Laclede in 1764 and named after King Louis IX (who is also the city's namesake). The current church was completed in 1834, and now sits in the shadow of THE ARCH. The New Cathedral is the Cathedral Basilica of St. Louis, seat of the archdiocese, located in the Central West End.

Provel: A processed cheese made by combining cheddar, Swiss, and provolone. St. Louisans love it on Imo's (pronounced EE-mos) pizza and sandwiches. Provel's prefab nature gives it a buttery taste and a gooey, greasy texture, easy to peel off a crust, less stringy than mozzarella. Pronounced pra-VEL. A Salsiccia is a sandwich with provel, pepperoncinis, and pickles with meat sauce on a sesame seed bun. A Prosperity sandwich is open-faced toasted garlic bread topped with roast beef and provel. A Gerber sandwich is an open-faced toasted hoagie with garlic butter, ham, and provel.

St. Paul Sandwich: An egg foo young patty, lettuce, pickle, and mayonnaise on white bread. Served in greasy Chinese take-outs.

Schoemehl pots: Planters made from lengths of sewer pipe, used as barricades to block off streets, with the goal of reducing traffic and crime. Named for former Mayor Vince Schoemehl.

Slinger: A breakfast plate consisting of two eggs and a beef patty on hash browns, smothered with chili, cheese, onions, and jalapenos. Best enjoyed very early in the morning, preferably at 2 a.m., as you're leaving the bar.

Sloo: St. Louis University, a Jesuit institution of higher learning. St. Louis University High School is "Sloo High."

The Stroll: A street where prostitutes troll for customers.

T-Ravs: Toasted ravioli.

U City: University City, a suburb which does not actually contain a university.

Umsul: The University of Missouri at St. Louis.

The Ville: Traditionally African American neighborhood on the North Side. Originally known as Elleardsville. Arthur Ashe, Chuck Berry and Tina Turner attended The Ville's Sumner High, a once-segregated school named for Massachusetts's abolitionist senator Charles Sumner.

Wash U.: Washington University in St. Louis, an elite private college. Pronounced "Worsh U." by older St. Louisans.

Washers: A game that involves pitching a doughnut-shaped metal disc at a box with a tube in the center. Landing the washer in the box scores one point, landing it on the tube scores three. Washers tournaments are regularly held in and around St. Louis. Also called "worshers," of course.

WISCONSIN

"77 Square Miles Surrounded by Reality": Madison, the state capital, home of the University of Wisconsin and stronghold of public radio, farmers' markets, Third World restaurants, alternative newspapers, and Volkswagens with "Visualize Whirled Peas" bumper stickers. While campaigning for governor in 1978, Lee Sherman Dreyfus declared that "Madison, Wisconsin, is 30 square miles surrounded by reality." Dreyfus was likely critiquing state government, but Madisonians have embraced the remark as a commentary on their rejection of mainstream values and ideas. In 2013, Mayor Paul Soglin suggested "77 Square Miles Surrounded by Reality" as Madison's official motto. (The city had more than doubled in size since Dreyfus's campaign.) It was not adopted, although Madison has adopted the plastic pink flamingo as its official bird. Among conservative Wisconsinites, "Madison" is shorthand for impractical liberalism. "I think it's pretty clear you have two different worlds in this state," Gov. Scott Walker once said. "You have a world driven by Madison and a world driven by everybody else in the state of Wisconsin."

Bakery: Baked goods. "We're goin' to get some bakery. You wanna doughnut?"

Bernie Brewer: The mascot of the Milwaukee Brewers, a mustachioed blonde character who slides down a chute in Miller Park whenever the home team hits a home run. The Brewers also entertain their fans with famous racing sausages. Stadium employees dressed as Bratwurst, Polish Sausage, Italian Sausage, Hot Dog, and Chorizo run around the basepaths. Needless to say, Bratwurst wears lederhosen.

The Birkie: The American Birkebeiner, a 50-kilometer-plus cross country ski race from Cable to Hayward.

Boughten: The past participle of "to buy." "I don't live in Sheboygan anymore. I have boughten a house in Manitowoc."

Brat: Pronounced "brot," it's short for bratwurst, a pork sausage that is the unofficial encased meat of Wisconsin. Sheboygan County is the bratwurst capital of Wisconsin, and, therefore, the world. Supermarket vestibules are papered with flyers advertising Brat Frys for the Kiwanis Club or an ailing child. Brats are also the culinary accessory for watching a Packers game. The beer brat—bratwurst simmered in ale or lager for half an hour—is a popular recipe, since it combines two unhealthy German obsessions.

The Bronze Fonz: A statue of *Happy Days* character Arthur Fonzarelli on the Milwaukee Riverwalk, giving his trademark thumbs-up gesture. *Happy Days* was set in Milwaukee, a city not known for Italian greasers. The show was created by Garry Marshall, who grew up in the Bronx, and Wisconsin native Thomas L. Miller. The two producers conflated their hometowns into a successful TV series. *Happy Days*'s most authentic Milwaukee touch was Arnold's Drive-In, which was based on the Milky-Way in Glendale, which Miller patronized as a teenager.

Bubbler: A drinking fountain, because in the original design, the water bubbled up from a central spout. The Kohler Co., a Wisconsin-based manufacturer of plumbing supplies, advertised one of its early models as having a "Vitreous China Non-Squirting Bubbler."

Bucky: Bucky Badger, mascot and personification of University of Wisconsin sports teams. When they win, fans shout, "Go Bucky!"

Budge: To cut in line.

Cheese Curds: Proof that Wisconsinites will eat *any* dairy product or *any* fried food. Cheese curds are misshapen lumps of cheddar in its early stage of development, before it ripens or sharpens. A finger-sized food, curds are ideal for snacking. Also called "squeaky cheese," because of the sound the curds make when bitten into. Fried cheese curds—curds dipped in batter or sizzled in oil—are eaten at the bar or the county fair. "Curdistan" is another nickname for Wisconsin.

Deer Camp: A place UP NORTH where men go to get away from their wives every November. There's a lot of beer drinking, a lot of dirty jokes, and not a lot of personal hygiene. If you shoot a deer, that's a bonus. During this same period, women go to doe camp, taking charter buses to shop in Chicago.

Drink Wisconsinbly: Drink excessively. When 24/7 Wall Street came out with a list of the 20 drunkest cities in America, 12 were in Wisconsin. (Appleton was number one, with 26.8 percent of adults reporting "drinking to excess.") When the *Onion* was published in Madison, its Page 3 pinup was a "Drunk of the Week." The World's Largest Six Pack is a sextet of beer tanks covered with LaCrosse Beer labels. Wisconsin has over 3,000 taverns — third per capita, after colder, more sparsely populated Montana and North Dakota, and also third overall (barely), behind California and New York.

FIB: Fucking Illinois Bastard, the Wisconsin equivalent of Michigan's FIP. Applied to Chicago-area tourists who mob Door County and the Dells every summer, clogging the two-lane county roads with gleaming SUVs, and asking mom-and-pop diner owners, "Do you have wi-fi?" "Have you been to that new microbrewery in Egg Harbor?" "Nah, it's full of FIBs." A FISHTAB is a Fucking Illinois Shithead Towing A Boat.

Fifty-Yard Line: State Highway 50, which runs past the Brat Stop in Kenosha, because it's the dividing line between Bears fans and Packer fans.

Fish Boil: The fish boil was invented by Scandinavian fishermen who poached their catch in potbellied stoves aboard gill-netters. The practice was brought on shore for church suppers and community picnics, and is now a Door County tourist attraction, combining comfort food, local color, and pyrotechnics. At the Viking Restaurant in Ellison Bay, the kettle is a 20-gallon Speed Queen washing machine tub above a wood fire. It's filled with water, salt, onions, potatoes, and fish. As the water bubbles and steams, the cook shouts "Boil on!" and tosses a cup of cooking oil on the flames, which blossom into an orange bonfire for a roaring instant, burning off the water's oily glaze. His assistants haul away the steaming vat. Served with cole slaw and rye bread off of aqua cafeteria trays, on a picnic table decorated with OLE AND LENA carvings.

Fish Fry: The Friday fish fry is served at churches, American Legion halls, and taverns in every Roman Catholic community. But Wisconsin puts a Germanic twist on it (as it does on everything). The traditional Wisconsin fish fry consists of a beer-battered freshwater fish—perch, smelt, bluegill, or walleye—with potato pancakes, rye bread, cole slaw, and tartar sauce. And beer. Meat on Friday is a sin, but never beer.

Fondy: Diminutive of Fond du Lac (pronounced "fonna lack.")

Hodag: A legendary creature with the head of a frog, the face of an elephant, sharp horns, and a spiked spine and tail. A hodag was allegedly captured in Rhinelander in 1893 by Eugene Shepard, a North Woods P.T. Barnum, who displayed his catch at county fairs for ten cents a peep. It was actually a wooden carving with bulls' horns, wired to shake when viewers approached. Shepard's sons provided the audio by howling from a hidden room. The hodag ate only white bulldogs, and could only be killed with lemons. Rhinelanders embraced the hoax, erecting a hodag statue outside the visitor center and naming the high school sports team the Hodags. The city's website insists that 90 percent of the golf balls lost in Rhinelander County are eaten by "the Hodag."

Hot Ham and Rolls: A Sunday after church/after hangover tradition at Milwaukee bakeries, taverns, and restaurants. Some give away free hard rolls with the purchase of a pound of ham, so customers can assemble their hot ham and rolls at home, while others serve straight-up mini sandwiches.

Kay Kay: Kinnickinnic Avenue in Milwaukee.

Killwaukee: Mordant nickname for Milwaukee, suggesting it's a Gomorrah or crime and murder. Milwaukee, which mostly avoided the blight and abandonment that afflicted other northern cities, is not terribly violent by the standards of urban America, but it is more violent than the rest of Wisconsin. Title of numerous rap songs.

Kringle: A flaky Danish pastry shaped like a giant doughnut. Consists of 32 layers of dough, filled with fruit or nuts. The Kringle capital is Racine, where a half-dozen bakeries serve it with coffee or ship it around the world to homesick SCONNIES.

Lambeau: Lambeau Field, the Green Bay Packers' stadium, which is located across the street from a strip mall in Ashwaubenon. Named for Curly Lambeau, the team's founder. Green Bay was one of numerous small Midwestern cities to host a franchise in the NFL's early years. Canton, Ohio, Rock Island, Ill., and Hammond, Ind., all lost their teams, but the Packers are still in Green Bay because the team was set up as a public trust, with the original stipulation that proceeds from its sale go to a local American Legion post. The Packers have a fan base throughout Wisconsin and the Upper Peninsula of Michigan, who refer to attending a game as "going to Lambeau." After a touchdown, players perform the "Lambeau Leap," jumping into the embrace of appreciative spectators.

Milwaukee Goiter: A beer belly. Also called a "tavern belly."

M'wahkee: The state's largest city. The 'l' is silent.

Mud Duck: A Minnesotan.

No/Not: Like EH, tag questions that encourage agreement or response. From the German *nicht*, which can appear the end of a sentence, as in *Sie arbeitet nicht* (She is not working). "It's getting cold today, no?" or "Brewers gonna have a good year this year, not?"

Over Dere: That place I'm pointing at.

Sconnie: Originally an insult for a Wisconsinite, based on the natives' pronunciation of their state's name: wi-SCAHN-sin, with a hard emphasis on the middle syllable, not wis-CON-sin, as a newscaster would say it. Now embraced as a term of state pride. Sconnie Nation, which produces Wisconsin-themed T-shirts (and copyrighted the word), describes Sconnie as "tailgating, bowling, BUBBLERS, washing cheese curds down with a beer, having a tractor-shaped mailbox, or eating a cream puff."

She: An inanimate object, often mechanical. "How's your chainsaw runnin'?" "Oh, she's runnin' pretty good."

Sheepshead: A five-handed card game played with the 7, 8, 9, 10, and face cards. A translation of the original German name *Schafskopf.*

Sidecar: A six-ounce glass of Miller Lite served with a Bloody Mary, to smooth out the taste.

Stallis: West Allis, a suburb of Milwaukee.

"Start with me last": Waiter, take everyone else's order before mine.

Stop-and-Go Light: A traffic signal. "Turn left at the next stop-and-go-light."

Sturgeon Spearing: Every winter, on Lake Winnebago, fishermen set up shanties and attempt to catch sturgeon by probing a five-pronged spear through a rectangular hole in the ice. Sturgeon spearing season lasts sixteen days, beginning the second Saturday in February. Even though Lake Winnebago is said to contain the world's largest population of freshwater sturgeon, most spearers come away disappointed: only 13 percent catch a fish, which can weigh up to 200 pounds.

Supper Club: A white tablecloth and candlelight restaurant that serves generous cocktails and even more generous helpings of prime rib or fried fish, always accompanied by a relish tray. Supper clubs overlook lakes or woodlands in resort towns, and employ easy listening combos to play pop standards. Unabashedly dated (that's part of the appeal), their architecture is best described as mid-century rococo: Moorish castles, pagodas, and plenty of neon. The supper club has its origins in the repeal of Prohibition, when the first liquor licenses were granted to rural establishments that served food.

Sweet or Sour?: Do you want Sprite or sour mix in your Old Fashioned?

Terrace: The grassy area between the sidewalk and the street. "When ya mow the lawn, don't forget to mow the terrace, too."

Tosa: Wauwatosa. "Wau" is an Algonquin phoneme that appears in the names of numerous Wisconsin cites: Milwaukee, Pewaukee, Wausau, Ashwaubenon, Waupaca. So nobody misses it when it's left out.

Tuna Quarter: Two dollars and twenty-five cents.

TYME Machine: An automatic teller machine. The acronym stands for Take Your Money Everywhere.

Uecker Seats: Obstructed view seats in the top row of the upper deck at Miller Park. Ticket price: one dollar. Named in honor of Brewers broadcaster and former big-league catcher Bob Uecker. In a 1980s Miller Lite commercial, an usher told Uecker his ticket was not for the box seat he was occupying. "Must be in the front row," he enthused, before finding himself exiled to the upper deck. One of the Uecker Seats is occupied by a statue of Bob in a blue sports shirt.

Ya Hey Dere!: Traditional Upper Midwestern greeting, now mostly used for comic effect, to suggest an overenthusiastic North Woods rube. In the 2000s, Budweiser filmed a Wisconsin-themed take-off on its "Wassup" ad. A man in bar called a friend and asked, "Ya hey dere, Vern. How's by you?" He then got calls from a deer hunter and a LAMBEAU tailgater, who both bellowed "Yah hey dere!" into the phone. Wisconsinites still answer the phone "yah," but leave out the "hey dere."

BIBLIOGRAPHY

Ash, Sharon, "The North American Midland as a dialect area." In *Language Variation and Change in the American Midland: A New Look at 'Heartland' English*, edited by Thomas E. Murray and Beth Lee Simon, 33-56. Philadelphia: John Benjamins Publishing Company, 2006.

Boberg, Charles. "The Phonological Status of Western New England." *American Speech* 76.1 (2001): 3-29.

Campbell-Kibler, Kathryn, and M. Kathryn Bauer. "Competing Reflexive Models of Regional Speech in Northern Ohio." *Journal of English Linguistics* Vol. 43 (2) (2015): 95-117.

Crotty, James Marshall. *How to Talk American: A Guide to Our Native Tongues*. New York: Mariner Books, 1997.

Donahue, Thomas S. "On Inland North and the Factors for Dialect Spread and Shift." In *"Heartland" English: Variation and Transition in the American Midwest*, edited by Timothy C. Frazer, 49-58. Tuscaloosa, Ala.: The University of Alabama Press, 1993.

Donahue, Thomas S. "On the eastern edge of the Heartland: Two industrial city dialects." In *Language Variation and Change in the American Midland: A New Look at 'Heartland' English*, edited by Thomas E. Murray and Beth Lee Simon, 105-128. Philadelphia: John Benjamins Publishing Company, 2006.

Fischer, David Hackett. *Albion's Seed: Four British Folkways in America*. Oxford: Oxford University Press, 1989.

Gordon, Matthew. *Small Town Values and Big-City Vowels: A Study of the Northern Cities Shift in Michigan*. Durham, N.C.: Duke University Press Books, 2000.

Herndobler, Robin. "Sound Change and Gender in a Working-Class Community." In *"Heartland" English: Variation and Transition in the American Midwest*, edited by Timothy C. Frazer, 137-156. Tuscaloosa, Ala.: The University of Alabama Press, 1993.

Johnstone, Barbara. *Speaking Pittsburghese: The Story of a Dialect*. New York: Oxford University Press, 2013.

Karlen, Neal. "If the Shoe (Snowshoe?) Fits, Well," *The New York Times*, May 5, 1996.

Labov, William, Sharon Ash and Charles Boberg. *The Atlas of North American English: Phonetics, Phonology and Sound Change*. Berlin: de Gruyter Mouton, 2005.

Labov, William. *Dialect Diversity in America*. Charlottesville, Va.: University of Virginia Press, 2012.

Linn, Michael D. "The Origin and Development of the Iron Range Dialect in Northern Minnesota." *Studia Anglica Posnaniensia* 21 (1988): 75-87

Loss, Sara Schmelzer. "Iron Range English long-distance reflexives." (Ph.D. diss., University of Minnesota, 2011).

Mohr, Howard. *How to Talk Minnesotan: Revised for the 21ˢᵗ Century.* New York: Penguin Books, 2013.

Murray, Thomas E. "Positive *anymore* in the Midwest." In *"Heartland" English: Variation and Transition in the American Midwest*, edited by Timothy C. Frazer, 173-186. Tuscaloosa, Ala.: The University of Alabama Press, 1993.

Murray, Thomas E. "The Language of St. Louis, Missouri: Dialect Mixture in the Urban Midwest." In *"Heartland" English: Variation and Transition in the American Midwest*, edited by Timothy C. Frazer, 125-136. Tuscaloosa, Ala.: The University of Alabama Press, 1993.

Purnell, Thomas, Eric Raimy and Joseph Salmons. *Wisconsin Talk: Linguistic Diversity in the Badger State*. Madison, Wis.: University of Wisconsin Press, 2013

Remlinger, Kathryn. "The Intertwined Histories of Identity and Dialect in Michigan's Copper Country." In *New Perspectives on Michigan's Copper Country*, edited by Alison K. Hoagland, Erik C. Nordberg, and Terry S. Reynolds, 73-86. Hancock, Mich.: Quincy Mine Hoist Association, 2007.

Thomas, Erik R. "A Longitudinal Analysis of the Durability of the Northern-Midland Dialect Boundary in Ohio." *American Speech*, Vol. 85, No. 4 (Winter 2010): 375-430.

Woodard, Colin. *American Nations: A History of the Eleven Rival Regional Cultures of North America*. New York: Penguin Books, 2012

ACKNOWLEDGEMENTS

This project grew out of an article on the Northern Cities Vowel Shift in *Belt Magazine*. Thanks to publisher Anne Trubek for seeing it had the potential to become a book, and thanks to editor Martha Bayne (who's been editing my writing since we both worked for the *Chicago Reader*), for helping to shape it, and for letting me tell the "Melvina, Paulina, and Lunt" joke. I would also like to thank another former *Reader* editor, Alison True, who asked me in 1998 to write lists of slang from Michigan, Indiana, Wisconsin, and Downstate Illinois for the newspaper's annual "These Parts" issue. Many of the terms I discovered then appear in this book.

I traveled all over the Midwest to research this book. Here's a list of people and places who helped me.

Buffalo: I first met steel industry historian Mike Malyak when I was researching my Rust Belt history, *Nothin' but Blue Skies*. We've kept in touch, and he met me for breakfast in Lackawanna to teach me some Buffalo slang, and to tell me that when he was in Air Force, Californians commented on the way he pronounced "box." Thanks also to Buffalo expat Mitch Gerber, Eileen Buckley and Brian Meyer from WBFO, and the staff and patrons of Nietzche's bar in Allentown.

Pittsburgh: I also met Daniel and Ellie Valentine when I was writing *Nothin' but Blue Skies*. They had breakfast with me in their now-closed Homestead restaurant, the Tin Front Café. Michele Saling, a Pittsburgh native, regaled me with colorful local slang, and Vince Guerrieri shared his insights from several years of living in the 'Burgh.

Ohio: In Cleveland, thanks to Christine Borne for letting me listen to her talk all these years, and to Dennis Kucinich, for responding "Come ahhhhn!" when I interviewed him for

Salon.com and asked him if he'd ever heard of the website. Also Jack Buehrer, who quoted me in his article, "The Origins and Evolution of the Cleveland Accent (Yes, You Have an Accent, Cleveland)." In Cincinnati, I visited Cincy Shirts and Homage, competing shops in Over the Rhine that sell T-shirts with local sayings such as "Where'd You Go to School?" and "Nobody Puts Cincy in a Corner." I also had dinner with in-laws Janet Ireland, Karen Cobb, and Sheryl Rottenberger, who taught me the nuances of "Please?"

Michigan: Detroiter Nikita Murray taught me the meaning of "What up, doe?" and Yooper Tom Bissell helped me understand the many meanings of "eh," and why Yoopers stop using it once they cross the bridge. Thanks also to the Flivv, the only Yooper on my dorm room floor at the University of Michigan, and Sam Coleman, who taught me to say "Holy Wah!"

Indiana: Amanda Temple and I worked together at *Lake* magazine, which had its office in LaPorte. She's a native Hoosier, from Hudson Lake, and taught me South Bend slang. I met Marsha Jannusch when I worked at the *Herald & Review* in Decatur, Illinois. She now lives in Vincennes, Indiana, and introduced me to the fricassee.

Illinois: The guys at my local bar, the Lighthouse Tavern in Rogers Park, taught me about the childhood game "pinners," and John Gorman, an Edgewater native and my former editor at the *Chicago Tribune*, told me it was called "ledge" in his day. Thanks to Jake Malooley for inviting me to write an article on the Chicago accent for the *Reader*, and to Bill Leff and Wendy Snyder for inviting me on to their WGN radio show to talk about it. And R.I.P. John Goritz, my racetrack buddy from Burbank, who used to shout "Dayt's awesome!" whenever I cashed a bet. You had a great Chicago accent, Johnny.

Iowa: Kim Brown, a native of Manchester and now a resident of Cedar Rapids, introduced me to some Iowans who were working out of the office she was running as an organizer for the Bernie Sanders campaign. I helped stump for Sanders in Iowa, but ended up voting for Chicago native Hillary Clinton, because we haven't had a president with an Inland North accent since Gerald Ford. Tom Snee taught me about Snake Alley, and David Burke, longtime entertainment columnist for the *Quad City Times*, gave me some details on Quad Cities style pizza.

Wisconsin: I've been learning Wisconsin's quirky culture for years, ever since I wrote a book called *The Third Coast: Sailors, Strippers, Fishermen, Folksingers, Long-Haired Ojibway Painters and God Save the Queen Monarchists of the Great Lakes*, a travelogue of a 5,000-mile trip around all five lakes. David Gumieny, proprietor of the World's Largest Barber Pole in Elkhart Lake, introduced me to brats. Marcy Skowronski, owner and grande dame of Milwaukee's Holler House, which contains America's oldest bowling alley, first served me hot ham and rolls. Thanks also to Jon Mark Bolthouse, a high school classmate who now runs the library in Fond du Lac, and Matt Thomas, who read my list of Wisconsin phrases.

Minnesota: Nowhere in the Midwest was I treated to warmer hospitality than in Brainerd, which I appreciated, because the temperature was 16 below zero when I arrived in January. At Kavanaugh's Resort, the Kavanaugh brothers taught me that Alexandra is "The Alek," and told me where to find a boiled dinner. Their handyman, Bobby Adams, took me ice fishing and told me the difference between breakfast, dinner and supper. At the Brainerd Lakes Curling Club, Dave Johnson introduced me to the rules of the game, and curling terminology. Dave Guenther, organizer of the Antique Snowmobile Rally in Pequot Lakes, invited me to the pre-rally potluck—which of course included hotdish and bars—then let me ride an old sled. That's Minnesota Nice.

St. Louis: Thanks first of all to Jeff and Randy Vines, owners of STL-Style, a shop specializing in T-shirts with St. Louis sayings. (Local T-shirt shops were a great resource for this book.) They taught me a ton of St. Louis slang, and even let me listen on a phone call with a friend who speaks the classic St. Louis accent. Thanks also to Kiara Bryant at the St. Louis Convention & Visitors Commission.

In addition to these local visits, I did a lot of research in taverns on the North Side of Chicago. The reason: Chicago is a magnet for Midwestern college graduates, and every Big Ten school has at least one bar catering to its alumni. So I mingled with Big Ten grads at McGee's (Ohio State), Will's Northwoods Inn (Wisconsin), Waterhouse (Purdue), Little Fort Tavern (Iowa), and Sluggers (Indiana). I also went to Sedgwick's, the St. Louis bar, and Durkin's, the Pittsburgh bar.

Thanks, all you guys!

ABOUT THE AUTHOR

Edward McClelland is the author of *Nothin' But Blue Skies: The Heyday, Hard Times, and Hopes of America's Industrial Heartland* and *The Third Coast: Sailors, Strippers, Fishermen, Folksingers, Long-Haired Ojibway Painters, and God-Save-the-Queen Monarchists of the Great Lakes*. His writing has also appeared in the *New York Times, Los Angeles Times, Columbia Journalism Review, Salon, Slate,* and the *Nation*.

59117582R00093

Made in the USA
Lexington, KY
23 December 2016

Worship Feast

100 Awesome Ideas for Postmodern Youth

Abingdon Press
Nashville

WORSHIP FEAST:
100 Awesome Ideas for Postmodern Youth

Copyright 2003 by Abingdon Press.

This book is printed on acid-free, recycled paper.

ISBN 0-687-06357-4

MANUFACTURED IN THE UNITED STATES OF AMERICA

06 07 08 09 10 11 12—10 9 8 7 6 5 4 3

Contents

Meet the Writers

Reverend Daniel S. White is Pastor of Worship and Worship Team Coordinator at Christ Church of Oak Brook, in suburban Chicago. Rev. White coordinates musicians, pastors, and technology staff so that Christ Church might experience God-exalting, people-engaging worship. He leads the worship staff in producing six worship services in three distinct expressions of worship (traditional/Reformed, praise/contemporary, ancient-future/contemplative). Rev. White is also the pastor for Sojourn, a missional community engaging in multisensory worship experiences. During his years as a youth pastor, he discovered a passion for communicating the gospel in authentic and engaging ways. Rev. White lives in Oak Brook with his wife, Lisha, and daughters, Sophie and Chloe. They enjoy the outdoors and In 'n Out Burgers.

Jonathon Norman serves as a United Methodist youth pastor in Nashville. He has participated in worship retreats and has a special interest in the needs and passions of postmodern young people. He is also a writer of poetry and song and has been published in *The Anthology of Christian Poetry*. He is a native of Nashville, where he lives with his wife and son.

Jenny Piper is the youth minister for Bethlehem United Methodist Church in Franklin, Tennessee. She is continually seeking new ways to engage youth in worship and point them to God by creating sacred spaces for holy encounters.

Jennifer A. Youngman is a development editor of youth resources for The United Methodist Publishing House. She recently spent a week at the Taizé community in France, singing, praying, meditating, and worshiping. She is passionate about creating space for young people to experience God in worship. She and her husband, Mark, live in Nashville, with their two dogs, Roxanne and Wrigley Field. (Go Cubs!)

Feast
On God's
Goodness

You have just opened an encyclopedia, a dictionary, a how-to guide, a workbook, and an index of worship ideas all in one. Make the words on these pages come alive in your worship spaces. Expand your understanding and concepts of worship so that you become even more intentional about meeting the worship needs of your youth. Don't settle for snack-food worship—feast on God's goodness in your worship!

So How Do You Get Started?

If you already have a youth worship service—

◇ Read the introduction ("Make Worship an Experience") and evaluate your current worship service or opportunities.

◇ Ask yourself these questions: Is your worship multisensory? Do your youth have some ownership of the service? Are the participants immersed in a God-experience in worship?

If yes, then supplement your service with some fresh ideas. If not, then incorporate some elements from Chapter One: Logistics and How To's. Then, add one or more ideas from the chapters on the senses. Try to engage all the senses in worship.

If you want to start a youth worship service—

◇ Gather together a youth worship ministry team—of actual youth—who will plan, direct, promote, and lead the services. Give the team members this book and let them use the ideas to put together their own services.

◇ Choose a time and a place that will attract the largest number of youth.

◇ Put together a group of instrumentalists— some youth, some adults.

◇ Don't worry about trying to be hip and edgy; just be authentic in your own community.

If you need ideas for short devotional times—

◇ Find a Scripture reference, a theme, or a particular sense that you want to focus on and match a worship idea with your devotional time.

◇ Give this book to some youth and let them develop and lead devotions based on an idea.

If you want to enhance your Sunday morning worship—

◇ Find some ideas that will easily fit into your Sunday morning liturgy or routine and talk them over with your senior pastor.

◇ Use the ideas to create an experiential worship service for your youth Sunday worship.

Make Worship an Experience

"Taste and see that the LORD is good" (Psalm 34:8).

A modern church's take on this psalm might more appropriately be "hear and see that the Lord is good"; but for the postmodern young person, the psalm is more like "taste and see and touch and hear and smell, in other words, experience that the Lord is good!" The acquisition and communication of knowledge are important issues for postmoderns—both are interactive experiences. Consequently, experiential worship is an imperative with which the postmodern church must grapple. So, what are the elements that create "experiential worship"?

Symbolism

While the written word still thrives, postmodern youth are also eager to experience truth and beauty through the use of symbols. Stained glass, banners, crosses, icons—these are rich symbols of our tradition through which God's beauty is manifested to us. Most modern churches use at least some of these symbols or even others; however, they are more static elements of worship rather than dynamic instruments for encountering the Living God. Consider the meaning found in capturing the beauty of the tradition and recasting those symbols in today's world. For instance, project images of saints or icons on a screen throughout worship, or even add some chant music that has been infused with a hip-hop beat. Postmodern youth value a connection to the past and find meaning in bringing the past into the current.

Multisensory

The table fellowship of the believers recorded in the Book of Acts was a sensory experience, not to mention the Temple worship found in Leviticus. According to Acts 2 they not only devoted themselves to the apostles' teaching, but also to sharing a meal together and praying for one another and meeting in the Temple. The image brings to mind, not individuals quietly filing into neat rows set up for them in a bare room, but people gathering together and learning from one another through interaction and dialogue. The picture is of a worshiping community that feasts together at God's table. Rather than just taking a single piece of bread and a small sip of wine as we do these days, they filled up on God's goodness.

To be multisensory in our worship is to be biblical. Dialogue about the Scriptures, lighting incense and candles, hearing testimonies, inviting liturgical dancers to share their gifts, allowing periods of silence—these are good places to start. In the modern era we have so capitalized on the cognitive aspects of worship that we have forgotten how to engage our other faculties in the worship of God. Fabric, flowers, candles, music, images, dance, food—surely these are part of a worship feast! Multisensory worship capitalizes on an ancient-future faith. This expression of worship utilizes the technology and resources of the current day in order to engage in ancient forms and movements of Christian worship.

Worship and Mission

To be biblical, the worshiping community must exist for more than the satisfaction of those individuals who attend. Worship is first and foremost about glorifying God through Jesus Christ. Through our worship, God fills us with Christian mission and purpose to bring forth the kingdom of God. Christian community without mission is self-serving; mission without Christian community is public service. Thus, individuals are propelled from the community experience to make a difference in their context of work, school, home, and so forth. So, if one is a follower of Jesus, the question is: What are we doing as an honest expression of our spirituality? To experience Jesus in a community of worship is an incredible thing, but the experience should motivate us to use our gifts and passions for the good of others and to our Lord's good pleasure.

Story

It has been said that the Word became flesh and we have turned him back into words. Yet Jesus was himself the master storyteller, and he didn't always *tell* a story simply to illustrate a point. The parable was used to truly communicate. In modern preaching and teaching, story was used to clarify an abstraction, to make an example, or to illustrate a moral. Yet the church of Jesus Christ has the ultimate storybook as its manual. The Bible is a great story from Genesis to Revelation about God and God's interaction with all creation and God's people.

Telling the story of the Scriptures will be a dominant approach to proclaiming the gospel in a postmodern context. To modern ears the term *story* tends to denote falsehood or myth. However, for the postmodern person story is reality, life-proven lessons, history and legacy, and something of true meaning. Or better, story is no different from the "facts" of the modern person. If science says one thing, it is acceptable for religion to say another. Paradox, in a postmodern context, is celebrated.

Community

Community exists for followers of Jesus before it is—or whether it is—experienced. The apostle John says that we have fellowship with one another because our fellowship is in the Son (1 John 1:3). In other words, it is not because we like one another that we have fellowship; it is a spiritual reality.

In his book *Life Together: Prayerbook of the Bible,* Dietrich Bonhoeffer says, "Christian community means community through Jesus Christ and in Jesus Christ. There is no Christian community that is more than this, and none that is less than this. . . . We belong to one another only through and in Jesus Christ." Surely this is the meaning of community for postmodern persons. Being "a community" involves more than being in the same place at the same time. Experiencing community is more than joining a small group. It has to do with pursuing common purposes and passions, living life, and doing worship together. Christian community is a God-infused sense of togetherness.

Characteristics of Postmodern People

◇ All about experience
◇ Deeply spiritual—longing for meaning/content
◇ Pluralistic/open-minded
◇ All-accepting—everything is relative
◇ Philanthropic/strong desire to help and give
◇ Community/tribal driven
◇ Aesthetically tuned-in—very creative
◇ Environmentally aware
◇ Globally minded
◇ Holistic—not willing to settle for compartmentalized faith
◇ On a quest for authenticity
◇ Relationships/relationships/relationships

Dig In!

So now you know why it is so very important to create awesome worship experiences for postmodern youth. While this book is not full of models to adopt in your youth ministries, the book is a collection of ideas for you to use to create postmodern worship experiences that are perfect for your group. The table is set, the food is prepared, the banquet awaits you—dig in to your worship feast!

1

Logistics & How To's

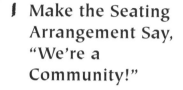

Notes

1 Make the Seating Arrangement Say, "We're a Community!"

The modern church often has relegated the faithful to sit in cleanly designed, orderly rows. Worship often involves staring at the back of people's heads rather than viewing the faces of the community that reflects the very image of the One we are worshiping. An ancient practice of the church is to gaze at the face of the fellow Christian because within the facial structure there is a resemblance of the cross. Thus, sitting in a circle or concentric circles is a simple way to remind worshipers of their interdependence and of the community to which God has called each of them.

Sit in a way that calls the worshipers to community by gathering in a circle, in a horseshoe fashion, or "in the round." Be intentional about the statement the worship space makes about your community of believers. Do you say "Welcome, welcome, welcome!" or "Sit down and don't look around"? All Christians long for authentic community, but postmodern students settle for nothing less.

2 Get Comfortable

Sit on rugs and pillows. Placing rugs and pillows around the worship space allows for flexibility in the design of the worship service. In this way, worshipers have some space to themselves, even while fully experiencing the community.

They can express their worship with their posture, or meditate without the distraction of someone sitting right next to them. They may also experience a sense of home in worship. Oftentimes the comfort we feel in different settings calls us to a sense of security and belonging. This comfort can be translated into a worship setting. The more at home we feel, the easier it is for us to set aside our distractions and truly commune with God.

Sitting on the floor is also reminiscent of gatherings in the Middle East. From ancient times forward, furniture was relatively sparse. In a transient culture it was simply impractical to take one's dinette set and lash it on a donkey. Using such casual seating also allows for the community to experience worship in a more casual setting.

Notes

Notes

3 Adapt Worship Tunes and/or Write Your Own

Not all worship songs are valuable for every community. A handful of songs usually get passed around throughout countries and between continents, but the best worship music is written by artists who are part of your worshiping community. In this way, musicians (including youth!) are offering their gifts before God just as the teacher or artist or tither does.

Imagine the richness of calling on your youth to write worship songs from within your specific situations. Not only does this call on their gifts, but also it gives a gift to the community in that your prayers in song are the actual needs and feelings of your particular group.

Also, many worship tunes overuse first-person singular and masculine pronouns. If community and diversity are values of postmoderns, then Christian praise and worship should focus less on "I, me, and my" and more on "us, we, and our" in the lyrics. Encourage the use of songs that do not use specifically masculine pronouns for both humanity and God. We are all God's children and should all find ourselves reflected in the message of music. And, God encompasses so much more than the sense of fatherhood. Let God be fully God through the music—Father, Mother, Spirit, Almighty, Friend, Advocate, Comforter, and all that God is.

✝ Get Down in Front!

Visually dissolve the separation between "up front" leadership and the worshiping community. Have the band or instrumentalists play from among the congregation rather than on a stage or platform. Another way to avoid the feeling of being "on stage" is to have them lead the music from behind the community— this way the instruments do not distract from the words of the music.

If a person is reading Scripture, have him or her sit among the worshipers. If a person is sharing a faith journey, have him or her sit on the opposite side of the room from the Scripture reader. Teach while physically walking among the community or even sitting with the group. All of these ideas help to dissolve the separation between leaders and laity that has so characterized much of the history of the church after the ancient community was established.

Notes

Notes

5 Don't Become Locked In to a Building

The early church was a flexible community. The exact place of the gathering of the faithful (that is, whose home was hosting the gathering) was unimportant. Instead, what was important was the presence of Christ by the Holy Spirit among his body of believers.

Revering space for worship was a much later development in the history of the church of Jesus Christ. Don't believe for one minute that you can enjoy a vibrant Holy Spirit experience only when you meet in a church building! That would be confusing the space for worship with God's holiness. God is holy everywhere. Get out there and worship God in all of creation.

Consider journeying to different churches or agencies for worship, especially in light of the missional opportunity. Go "out" and worship in a non-church building where the community of faith is thoroughly available to the general public. Another option is to meet in an underutilized church at a time that is convenient for the host; make a donation to the church, and leave it cleaner than when you got there. In this way the gathering can truly celebrate community as the Body of Christ.

6 Teach Creatively From the Bible

The Bible is a great manual for teaching creatively. Just think of the many ways God spoke to people—through a burning bush, by a pillar of fire, by sending a flood—to name just a few.

Be multisensory as you teach the Bible. If water is involved in the Scripture lesson, make opportunities to touch or taste water. If fire is a part of the story, then sit around a blazing fire for a message. If there's a slingshot in the story, allow the youth to practice with an actual slingshot (with soft pellets, of course!). Open up the Bible to your group.

Also there are myriad expressions of spirituality in contemporary life. "Faith" is a hot topic in the West. Followers of Jesus must gather together and unapologetically express a Bible-based worship that is dependent on what God has revealed in the Christian Scriptures. Move away from the modern love affair with thin "how-to" sermons that are attempts at self-help and consumer-oriented topical sermons aimed at entertainment rather than offering a Christian worldview. Teaching what the Bible actually says is authentic proclamation.

Notes

Notes

7 Deal With the Tough Stuff

The Bible is not a simple document. Different faith communities vary wildly on issues of biblical authority and all the ensuing doctrines. Whether you disregard a difficulty in the text as a scribal gloss or explain it as God's intended phraseology, it is dishonest for us in any cultural context to shy away from those passages that are not tidy or that seem culturally offensive. Those who are not followers of Jesus in a postmodern context are waiting for someone in a church who will honestly grapple with what the Bible says (and doesn't say).

The truth is that some stories in the Bible are not pretty and do not have a simple explanation. Easy answers for difficult passages are unacceptable for postmodern worshipers. They are happy to live in the tension and experience God's revelation through the passage without having an "answer." Feel free to say "I don't know" and to enter into dialogue with youth over the tough stuff. Engage the passages together through study and prayer. Be an example of authenticity.

8 Celebrate Diversity

Every worshiping community is comprised of different individuals with a different history and different points of view. This diversity can be both a blessing and a challenge. In a postmodern context there is a high tolerance for diversity and a true celebration of differences. The community of faith is called to celebrate the diversity found within the gathered followers of Jesus. The community of faith is also called to be accepting of those spiritual explorers who are coming to observe the worship experience.

In some senses, it is much easier to train yourself to live out the gospel of Jesus by accepting individuals for who they profess to be. It is, however, quite another thing for the community of Jesus-followers to allow for and truly celebrate diversity within the community. Show diversity in worship leadership. Have both guys and girls involved in leadership roles. Strive to incorporate ideas from different Christian traditions and various ethnic communities. Invite different churches to worship with you and merge your worship styles. Celebrate the God that is worshiped in various ways.

Notes

Notes

9 Change Constantly!

A sense of the ancient has great value in a postmodern context. Ancient practices in postmodern worship gatherings are welcomed and celebrated. That said, the exact same service over and over will bore youth into apathy in worship.

Change the worship styles nearly every week to keep interest high. Have a relatively normal service one week, followed by an immersion worship experience the next. Use art one week and food the next. Have an all-out praise and worship service one week and a quiet, meditation service the next. Don't keep the same basic format and just use different music—that approach won't provide the contrasting style that you are seeking.

Instead, continually change your format, your worship space, and the tone of the service. Pay close attention to what is going on in the lives of your youth and plan services that meet specific needs. Make changes to be as authentic to your group as possible.

10   Be Seeker-Sensitive

Although the "seeker-sensitive" church service movement has been criticized as consumer-driven and biblically thin, this movement has also taught the entire church a new language and provided an example of realized evangelism. In a postmodern context, celebrating an authentic, Christ-centered religious experience is in-and-of-itself seeker-sensitive.

However, the spiritual explorer still needs to have as many interpretive clues as possible for what is occurring in the worship gathering. Have designated people welcoming persons to the gathering and being available afterward for newcomers. Handouts explaining the values of the community are also interpretive tools. Such handouts can be the bearer of valuable information bringing theological and historical perspectives on the elements of the worship experience. Do all you can to think through the elements of the gathering through the eyes of the postmodern spiritual explorer. You may not need to adapt the gathering. But be sure to interpret it for newcomers.

Notes

Notes

11 Avoid Religion-Bashing

In a postmodern context, to unfairly criticize another's conviction is unproductive. Postmodern students are keenly aware of the difference between advocating for one's religious conviction and elevating ones' religious convictions by denigrating another's. Spend more time describing God and the Scriptures than describing other religions or persons negatively. If Christianity is truly the most winsome religion out there, then young people will see that as it is lived and articulated before them. Simply saying Christianity is better by comparison doesn't go a long way for the postmodern student.

Postmodern students celebrate diversity and authenticity. Use their enthusiasm to wrestle with issues of pluralism and a global society.

12 Celebrate Mystery

In modernity we tried to figure everything out. A postmodern context allows for, even craves, mystery.

Not only does the Christian tradition have ancient and contemporary streams of mysticism, but we also have a rather challenging book in the Bible. While seminaries teach courses on the Bible, the rest of us tend to scratch our heads and wonder what it means that Jesus is "with us always." What does it mean to "remember" in the Lord's Supper? Why are we supposed to worship? What does it mean to speak of God as the Trinity? These are all questions that people can answer to different degrees. But there are no simple answers to them, and to respond to these questions with simplistic answers is to be dishonest.

Postmodern followers of Jesus don't necessarily want to conquer the answers to these questions. They want to gain experience and wisdom, to wrestle with the questions and settle into the mystery that there will be questions without answers.

Notes

Notes

13 Be Multisensory

You need only to casually peruse the Book of Leviticus to understand that worship as understood in the Hebrew Scriptures was not just a thinking endeavor. The table fellowship of the believers recorded in the Book of Acts was also a sensory experience. According to Acts 2 they not only devoted themselves to the apostles' teaching, but to sharing a meal together and praying for one another and meeting one another in the Temple. The image is much more than individuals quietly filing into neat rows set up for them in a bare room. It is a picture of people gathering together and learning from one another through interaction and dialogue; it was eating together, not just taking a single piece of bread and a small sip of wine; they feasted! Food, sights, sounds, and smells have always been a part of the worshiping community.

Go out of your way to provide multisensory learning opportunities for your group. By connecting teaching moments to the senses, you will make the Bible and the faith come alive for the youth.

14 Don't Be Afraid of Theology

Worship must be more than for the experience. Theological conviction should drive the planning of community worship (not just what's easiest or what "works" at another church). The center of community worship is God; the purpose of worship is primarily God-exaltation, and second, empowering Jesus-followers for ministry.

Worship is not merely a self-help experience. Thus, in a postmodern context, it is important to know the rationale behind the elements used in worship. Be explicit about the theology behind symbols and imagery. Use ancient liturgies that are rich in language about the mystery of God. Write a liturgy from the perspective of the theology of your community and help the participants understand why they believe what they believe.

Youth are hungry to understand why we do what we do in worship and are starved to wrestle with theology. Worship is a perfect opportunity to feed their souls while engaging them in theology.

Notes

Notes

15 Know the Subculture of Your Community

We can glean much from the many excellent worship and evangelism ideas all around the globe. Several ministries in Britain, Canada, and the United States are experiencing a tremendous sense of God's blessing as they minister to postmoderns in their contexts.

The rest of us benefit because we can visit their churches, see their services on streaming webcasts, and seek out their leaders for wisdom. The potential downfall is that we sometimes attempt to take what is valuable to their worshiping community and try to transplant it to our own.

The harsh reality to be discovered is that subcultural context is staggeringly important—what works in Seattle won't necessarily work in your area. Avoid being trendy, but strive to be authentic. Tweak other worship models to fit your context.

Go to *www.theooze.com* to find a state-by-state listing of churches that are meeting the needs of postmodern worshipers.

16 Meet at a Unique Time

The church of Jesus Christ has traditionally met on the "Lord's Day" (Sunday) because it is the day that Jesus was raised from the dead; it was also the day when the Holy Spirit empowered the church at Pentecost. However, the sabbath was still celebrated on Saturday. For centuries the church met on a workday, not on a day devoted to worship. The believers met every day to worship in the Temple. So, Sunday is not the only biblical day when Christians can worship. Choose a special time that is unique to your community, as if to say "This is your time with God." Meet at midnight on Friday nights, or for breakfast during the week. Decide together as a community on a meaningful time that makes the worship all the more special.

17 Get Circular

Worship in a circle instead of rows as a symbol of unity, completeness, and eternity. When you sit in a circle, help the youth understand that they are not just randomly seated, but rather they are sitting in a pattern that represents the bond and connectedness you share as a group. If your space does not allow for sitting in a circle for the duration of the worship time, then move to a circle for the benediction. Be intentional about forming a circle of friendship and peace and accountability.

Notes

2

Visuals

Notes

18 Let the Worship Space Be a Visual in Itself

Be intentional about the worship space environment. The worship space in the ancient church was embellished with images, scents, and architectural grandeur.

Similarly, the postmodern context in which followers of Jesus presently live and work and breathe yearns for a synthesis of that which is ancient reintegrated with that which is "new." Approach the environment of worship in a postmodern context—with an eye toward the historical experience of the communion of saints while training the other eye on current means by which the community can take every thought captive and make it obedient to Christ (2 Corinthians 10:5).

Use the latest technology to capture a sense of the ancient. If you have stained glass windows, shine lights onto them to bring them into the worship focus. Go out of your way to create a worship environment that says, "This is a special place; something sacred happens here."

19 Hand Out "Fragments"

The concept behind fragments is based on the ancient church. The Bible as we know it today began as pieces of stories, letters, speeches, and poetry that were passed around among communities of believers. Sometimes the complete written work was not available, so "fragments" of Scripture passages were read.

One key element of using fragments is that they were not for private reading, study, or interpretation of Scripture—they were meant to be used as a communal experience. In fact, the Bible consists of Scriptures that were deemed useful for the community. Those Scriptures that did not get read in the community did not get canonized.

Hand out the Scripture lesson as a fragment, printed on a sheet of paper without numbered verses to preserve the narrative quality of the text. Distribute the items sealed with the intention that the individuals in the community should open the fragments only for reading when there is at least one other person with whom to read the Scripture. Illuminate the Bible lesson by adding this sense of mystery and by connecting to the early church.

Notes

Notes

20 Have a Progressive Nativity

Every week in Advent, add pieces of the Nativity a few at a time. Let the anticipation build as each piece finds its place around the manger. Talk about the symbols as they are placed in the worship space. Invite the youth to secretly move the pieces throughout your room as if the pieces are on a journey. This progression can be a fun way to excite the youth about the coming of the Christ Child.

Consider encouraging the youth to collect Nativity figurines from different cultures and art styles. Powerful symbolism builds when the figures around the manger are different colors, sizes, and shapes. Once all the different pieces are around the manger, have a discussion about what it must be like in the kingdom of God when cultures and colors are not a mark of separation, but of unity as people of God.

orship feast Worship feast rship feast

2 J Dim the Lights

The ancient church met in basements, other dark places, and cemeteries. Most of the time, gathering in the name of Jesus involved an element of danger. Needless to say, early Christians did not have electrical lighting. A sense of anticipation and urgency surrounded the early church. Capture that sense by drawing the lighting into the elements of worship.

Create a sense of excitement in worship with the lighting. Worship in candlelight or with dim lights. It may also be appropriate for you to worship with lights turned on brightly (for instance, at Easter). Think about the type of worship service you are planning and be intentional about making meaning in the lights. If you're having a prayer service, cover the altar in candles; if you're having a sunrise Easter service, let as much light in as possible.

Think about what candlelight says to you as you enter—it says, "This place is special," and "Something sacred is happening."

Notes

Notes

2-2 Experience the Word Visually

Expand your group's idea of what it means to "hear" the Scriptures. Move beyond the aural, and experience the Word as an event. When we see God's handiwork in nature, in the faces of others, in art, in acts of reconciliation, in the healing of broken relationships, God speaks to our hearts. We hear God in our hearts while experiencing God with our eyes.

Find ways to connect an image to the Scripture lesson and use it in meditation. Create image-based Scripture lessons by using silent dramatic presentations, slide shows, silent videos, and so forth.

2-3 Project Images

In a return to the ancient, a postmodern context develops people's ability to learn and comprehend knowledge through non-verbal means. Have a scrolling slide show projected of explicitly religious images (icons, crosses, saints, churches, and so forth) and implicitly religious images (pictures of nature or pictures that symbolize the theme of the night, children, persons in other countries, and so forth). Reminiscent of Celtic theology, image-based proclamation helps us move beyond only hearing words, to experiencing messages through pictures.

The images are not necessarily an active part of the service in that they may never be specifically pointed to. They are more of a supportive element that is a witness to the Word while all other aspects of worship are going on. Less theological but of importance is the fact that learning is not a linear experience for most "native" postmoderns, so the visual imagery as background keeps them engaged.

24 Proclaim the Good News

Jesus proclaimed the good news wherever he went whether he was speaking, healing, touching, or otherwise. The fact of the matter is that Jesus did more than talk—his "good news" is more than just words! He spat on the ground, he ate with people, he drew in the dirt, he healed the lame, and he read aloud the Scripture without making three application points. Move beyond down-loading theology to your group through words. Proclaim the gospel of Jesus Christ through drama, through silence, through actions, through dance. Convey that the news is not just average—it's great news!

Notes

Notes

25 Create a Community Altar

Invite the youth each week to bring items that represent what they desire to bring to God. Some weeks they may bring a symbol of joy and other weeks they may bring an object that is representative of a need. Let these symbols become the altar paraments.

Create a litany each week that helps the participants find meaning through the visual of a community altar. For example, if there has been a tragedy in your community, invite the youth to bring objects that represent how they are coping with the event or a symbol of how they see God working through the tragedy.

Then have a responsive reading that invites the youth to say aloud what their symbols represent—"I brought to the Lord a backpack full of burdens because I know that Jesus will carry the burden of 'this situation' if I let him."

Then the community responds, "God, our hearts are broken; but we know that you are still God."

26 Let the Communion Table Make a Statement About Who You Are

Place the altar or Communion table in the center of the worshiping community. In most churches the Communion table is situated at the front of the church on a chancel or stage. This "up front" status is different from having the table accessible to the worship community. When one walks into a worship space and sees that the entire room is situated around a Communion table with a loaf of bread and cup on it, there is no doubt that this table is integral to the worship experience. It is another way to heighten the theological reality of the centrality of the Lord's Supper by visual means.

27 Give Gifts

Give the youth a palm-sized object that relates to the theme of your worship and encourage them to hold it throughout the worship time. They can use the object for prayer and meditation. Also they will have a visual to take away with them that will help them reflect on their experience of worship.

Notes

Notes

2 8 Dance for the Lord!

Incorporate dance into the worship service. Dance is not only a biblical part of worship, but also a striking reminder of God's pleasure in beauty and art. The psalms have us dancing for joy in praise of God. Reclaim this beauty and artistry for the church as a powerful method of proclaiming the gospel message in the worship gathering.

Have a liturgical dancer or dance group give a testimony, offering, or response to the message through movement. Some would hear "liturgical dancers" and think only of a ballet company coming in to dance to a more classical piece of music, but dance can be much more in worship. Invite your group to create a liturgical dance to their favorite songs—from Kirk Franklin's music to DC Talk to worship music or even hymns. Look for workshops on liturgical dance in your area to get started.

100 Awesome Ideas for Postmodern Youth

29 Get Artsy

Have an artist from your group paint a picture as a witness to the message or Scripture reading. The artist works much the same way as the scrolling images by giving an authentic gift to the worshiping community. Utilize the gifts of your group by inviting different artist-type youth to draw, sketch, or paint throughout the worship service as a testimony. Sometimes you may want to incorporate an interview with the artist into the message, though the art in itself is testimony enough.

The purpose of having an artist paint in worship is twofold: 1. To present art as proclamation (the artist is proclaiming the gospel through his or her medium); 2. To present art as a Spirit-led response to the praise and worship, to the Scripture reading and teaching, to the silence, to Communion, and so forth. What an awesome way to fully utilize the gifts of your group!

30 Close Your Eyes

Plan a worship experience where the participants are blindfolded for the entire time. Focus on how blind we can be to others in need, or how dependent we are on God's guidance.

Notes

Notes

31 Commune With the Saints

Give handouts and project quotations from the saints. Celebrate the history of worship *in* worship. As Christians, we proclaim that we worship in the communion of saints living and dead. Using the wisdom and depth of the faithful throughout history is a valuable way to be challenged and to connect with the past. For instance, pray some prayers of Saint Francis or Mother Teresa. Read aloud together the writings of Julian of Norwich or Martin Luther King, Jr., as affirmations of faith.

A great way to include the saints (young and old) in your church is to videotape persons within your congregation and community talking about their faith. You could also have some people from outside the "youth group" write prayers for you to say together in your worship times.

32 Get Liturgical

Traditional liturgy has been tried and tested for both theological content and devotional meaningfulness. Liturgies aren't just for the "high church." All Christians can experience God through rich ancient texts and current prophetic voices.

Using liturgies (responsive readings, litanies, unison prayers, call and answer, reciting creeds, and so on) is a way to engage the youth through their participation in the readings and prayers. Look to ancient and modern liturgies to guide the development of the worship service.

Invite the participants to write responsive readings or unison prayers about specific circumstances in your community. Encourage the prophetic witness of your youth by having them write and lead litanies.

Notes

Notes

33 Color Your Space

Color associated with liturgical seasons can stimulate the imagination and senses especially if the significance is explained and built upon. Place a cloth on the altar that will become a large colored banner that the youth can draw or write on. During a special season such as Lent or Advent, send out invitations to the students to come to the worship experience dressed in the liturgical color.

For reference, the colors for holy days are: Advent—purple or blue; Christmas—white or gold; Season after the Epiphany—green; Lent—purple, with no color on Good Friday and Holy Saturday; Easter—white or gold; Pentecost—red; Season after Pentecost—green.

34 Light a Christ Candle

Have a candle that represents the light of Christ in the center of your worship space as a permanent reminder that Christ is always present. In liturgical churches the light of Christ is brought into the worship space to burn during the worship service and then is carried out as a sign that Christ's light is going out into the world.

You don't have to be part of a high-church tradition to capture the significance of Christ's light in your worship times. Invite different members of the group to light the candle each week, and to carry the light out from the center of the room and into the world.

35 Create a Living River

Create a small and shallow river in your worship space by laying a tarp down and lifting the sides with bricks. Scatter rocks or sand along the bottom of the tarp to give it the look of a river. Have the sound of a flowing stream playing as background for the service. (You will need a wet-vacuum for cleanup.) Center your theme around a Bible lesson on water. Have a time for the youth to walk in the water and feel the water on their feet or hands.

Notes

Notes

36 Videotape the Message

Tape yourself giving a message in different locations and in different settings. Then during worship, show the video instead of giving the message in person. Postmodern youth are such media-driven people that they will instantly connect with the image-based messenger.

Another way to use video is to go downtown or to malls and interview people about the topic with which you want to deal. You will no doubt get some crazy comments, but you will also likely get some profound words from unsuspecting shoppers or business persons.

You could also give some youth the videocamera and let them create a message. Some youth will want to make a short movie, while others will try a question-and-answer, interview-style message. Unleash the wisdom in your youth by inviting them to be the "preacher."

37 Light Candles as the First Act of Worship

The Christian community has often used candles as a reminder of the light of Christ and simply out of necessity. Candles have been and continue to be a meaningful part of worship services. Use candle lighting to call the community to worship by having the youth take a small candle, light it from a single lit candle on the altar, and go around the worship space lighting other candles. Fill the room with light until the room takes on a holy glow.

Lighting candles at the beginning of worship is also a way for each participant to signify his or her presence in worship. Incorporate a litany with the candle lighting that calls youth to light candles as a way of saying, "I'm here to worship you, God."

Notes

3

Tastes & Smells

Notes

38 Create a Temple Experience

You will need meat, a grill, fuel for the grill (a wood fire is recommended, if possible), and incense. You may want to add other details such as holding the worship in a tent, including readings or canticles in Latin or Hebrew, and so on.

Before the youth arrive, build a wood fire just outside the worship area (or in the worship area if you are using an outdoor space or tent). Set the meat on the grill a few minutes before the beginning of worship so that it will begin to cook as the youth are entering the worship area. Also, light several sticks of incense around the worship space.

For an even more intense sensory experience, you may want to have flour frying in oil over the fire as well. All these smells are things that we know to be part of the worship experience of Jewish people in the time of Jesus. Burnt offerings were made each day, so the smell of meat cooking was constant, incense was often burnt during worship, and the scent of flour and oil cooking is mentioned in the Bible as an aroma that was offered to God.

This potpourri of smells will work to give the participants an impression of what church was like in the days of the ancient Temple.

39 Fill the Worship Space With Holy Fragrance

Early Hebrew Temple worship (and earlier tabernacle worship) must have been a phenomenally multisensory experience. Besides the bleating, lowing, and chirping of the sacrificial animals, imagine the staggering amount of bloodiness and the smell of burning flesh. In the midst of all this fire and flesh was a beautifully decorated worship environment with golden lampstands and burning incense. (Stop anywhere in Leviticus and you're pretty much sure to find some kind of smell in worship.)

Demonstrate to the youth the connection with our Hebrew roots by burning incense during worship. Give the worship space a scent that the participants will remember whenever they smell a similar fragrance. Let the aroma permeate the worship space so that the worshipers will use their sense of smell to reflect on God's beauty. Using incense is also a way in which Christians can lay hold of a valued expression in the culture and claim it in the worship of Jesus. Malachi 1:11 says that in every place incense is offered to God to declare God's greatness. Bring incense into your worship space as both an offering to God and a sign of God's greatness among the nations.

Notes

Notes

A recipe for manna, based on the limited description in Exodus and other information can be found at *www.stratsplace.com/rogov/israel/manna_breakfast.html*.

40 God Provides

Offer youth a chance to taste what Scriptures describe manna to be like. No one knows for sure what it was that God provided for the wanderers, but we can taste something similar by following the descriptions of manna in Exodus 16:1-33 and Numbers 11:7-9. You will need some type of flatbread or wafer, honey, and coriander seed.

Lead the youth in a guided meditation about what the experience of the Hebrew people may have been like by asking them to close their eyes and think about the answers as you ask these questions:

• Have you ever been to the desert? If not, have you ever been to a deserted place? Think about that place for a moment. Try to imagine how you felt the first time you saw an expanse of wilderness.
• What might you need if you were going to stay there overnight? How would you prepare for a week?
• Now imagine you are on a journey in the wilderness. Every day you travel, but the journey never seems to end. Your supplies get low. What do you do?
• You are still on the journey. Days turn into weeks, weeks into months, months into

years. Your supplies have been consumed, lost, or just completely worn out. You are living off the land, but it is a desert. From day to day, you never know if you will find food or water. How do you feel?

- You pray to God to take you back home. You pray for relief from your hunger, from your aching feet, from your utter weariness. Do you cry to God in anguish? Do you beg? Do you get angry with God? How do you feel?

As the youth begin to vividly imagine the hunger of the Hebrew people, have volunteers quietly set in front of the youth pieces of the "manna" you have made. Allow them to eat as someone reads aloud the Scripture lessons about God's provision for the wanderers.

∜ Eat From the Land

During Advent you will more than likely tell the story of John the Baptist and his crazy tastes in food. When you cover the story this time, hand out gummy worms (to represent locusts—unless your youth will actually eat locusts) and honey-flavored candies and talk about John's unconventional ways as documented in Mark 3:4.

Notes

Notes

You will need a bread machine, an electrical extension cord, an outlet, and ingredients for your favorite bread recipe.

#2 Bake Bread in Worship

Look up Exodus 29:18, 25, 41; and 2 Corinthians 2:15. Each Old Testament Scripture refers to burnt offerings and how the aroma of such an offering is pleasing to God. In the New Testament reading, Paul explains to the Corinthians that they are, to God, the aroma of Christ among those who are being saved. This parallel between the aroma as an offering and followers of Christ being the aroma of Christ to God makes an interesting image for a life of sacrifice.

Place a bread machine on or near the altar table. Assemble the ingredients for the bread and set the machine so that the bread will begin baking as the youth enter the worship area. Many bread machine recipes have times specific enough that you should be able to time the baking pretty easily. Instruct different readers to read each of the Scriptures listed above. Then explain the significance of these Scriptures in your own words. You may also want to have various Scriptures posted in writing around the worship area projected on screens around the room.

Ask the youth, "Have you ever noticed how a particular smell can overtake a place or even change your mood? The first Scriptures that we read tell us that people gave burnt offerings because they believed the aroma was pleasing to God. A wonderful scent, like the bread we can smell now, fragrant flowers, or coffee brewing can permeate a whole environment. Less pleasing aromas, such as a skunk or diesel fumes, can also overwhelm an area and evoke entirely different reactions. What kind of aroma are you to God?" You may want to use the freshly baked bread to lead into Communion during this worship service, or simply enjoy the bread together.

⊬3 Bread for the World

Celebrate Communion around the world by using bread recipes that represent different countries and customs. Have several different loaves of bread decorating the altar and let youth take a piece from each loaf as they take Communion.

For instance: Spicy tea bread could represent Christians in Ethiopia. Pita bread connects us to the Middle East. Corn bread is representative of Native American meals. Banana bread could be offered as a reminder that Jamaica is not just a resort Island, but also a place where poverty and homelessness abound.

Notes

100 Awesome Ideas for Postmodern Youth

Notes

�F�F The Party Must Go On!

You will need party invitations (old and new); lots of food (finger foods, sandwiches, pizza, or your group's favorite "feast" foods); appropriate music; and anything else you might want for a celebration.

Have someone read aloud Luke 14:16-24. Then say something like: "Jesus likens the kingdom of God to a great party. When the host invites guests, many of the intended guests decline. Maybe some have other obligations; maybe some just don't feel like going to a party. The Scripture doesn't provide reasons. Many hosts would just cancel the event or decide to postpone, but not the party planner in this story. Instead, the host scours the streets, inviting all, letting everyone know that the party must go on.

"The kingdom of God is like that, because, whether or not we choose to accept it, God's grace is out there. God's grace has always been there, even before we knew about it, like an invitation waiting to be read. It is up to us to accept—to RSVP. Whether we go or not, the party is going on! God already loves us. When we accept the invitation, then we can begin to join the party, to celebrate the joy of basking in God's love.

Worship feast
Worship feast
Worship feast

"I would like to invite you to respond to this message by joining us in a celebration of God's love. If you want to outwardly acknowledge God's invitation, then come feast at God's table."

Bless the food and invite the participants to stay and feast in honor of God and in celebration of knowing God's amazing love.

45 Designate Gatherings for the Lord's Supper

Make celebrating Communion a big deal for your group. Some churches observe the sacrament every Sunday while others have Eucharist only once in a while. Whenever you have Communion, avoid tacking it on at the end of the service. Direct all other worship elements to culminate in celebrating Communion.

However you tell the story, whether through a "Great Thanksgiving" or by simply reading the story of the Last Supper, be intentional about saying what you are doing and why. Linger in the mystery of the ritual and feast on the goodness of the Lord.

Notes

Notes

⊬6 Tormented in the Flame

You will need Atomic Fireballs™ or other red-hot candy, a pitcher of cool water, and cups. Instruct the participants to take a piece of the candy and hold it in their mouth for as long as they can. As the youth eat the candy, have someone read aloud Luke 16:19-31, the story of poor man Lazarus (as an alternative, sing or play a recording of the spiritual "Poor Man Lazarus").

After the reading, explain to the worshipers that they are experiencing a sensation similar to that felt by the rich ruler in the story. Pour a cup of cold water from the pitcher you have prepared and say, "During his suffering, the ruler asked Lazarus to show him mercy with cool water when he had not himself shown mercy. Do you recall times when you have failed to be merciful to others?"

Offer an example of a time you failed to show mercy and give the youth a chance to tell their own examples if they feel comfortable doing so. Due to the sensitive nature of this topic, do not pressure anyone to participate in this discussion. You may want to offer general examples of ways we fail to show mercy (ignoring a beggar, not forgiving a friend, being unkind to a sibling).

Invite the youth to come to the altar by saying, "As Christians, we are called to relieve the suffering of others. As you come to the altar, take time to confess to God the times you have failed to show mercy and ask God to reveal to you opportunities to show mercy to others. If you wish, take a cup of cold water as a symbol of God's mercy on us."

*7 Have a Maundy Thursday Seder Meal

Many Christian traditions have begun participating in Seder meals during Lent and some specifically on Maundy Thursday. By connecting the history of our faith to the death and resurrection of our Savior, we linger on the promise that God had a plan for us from the beginning. Seder meals include a variety of different foods, smells, drinks, and a ceremonial hand-washing service—talk about multisensory! The meal is conducted with a precise order of service as to how things are supposed to occur. In fact, the word *Seder* means "order" and refers to the sequence in which different elements of the meal happen.

Notes

Find detailed instructions for hosting a seder meal at *www.cresourcei.org/ haggadah.html.*

Notes

48 The Real Thing

You will need several scented candles as well as the "real" things that inspired each of the candle scents. Set up several stations around the worship area with a lit candle and the item that corresponds to each candle. Some good examples: a peach-scented candle and a bowl of fresh, sliced peaches; a pine-scented candle and a bowl of pine needles; a cake-scented candle and a slice of cake; a lemon-scented candle and real squeezed lemon juice. Be creative in your choices. The important thing here is that the scented candle doesn't smell exactly like the real thing. (Vanilla and peppermint candles tend to smell so similar to their inspirations that they don't work well for this illustration.)

As the participants begin to enter the worship area, ask them to visit the stations around the worship area, taking time to smell each of the candles and the various other items. The youth may take time for prayer during this portion of the worship as well.

Once all have gathered and taken in the various scents, read aloud Deuteronomy 13:1-4; 1 Peter 1:18-25 and ask if they have ever confused something artificial with the real thing. Offer an example of a time you were fooled (mistaking a diet or one-calorie soda for a regular one in a taste test). Explain that it can be easy to confuse other things with true devotion to God. While some things look and smell a lot like the real thing, they can actually keep us from God if we become too devoted to them. Ask the youth to think about the things in their lives that may be holding them back from a closer relationship with God. Give the youth another chance to visit the scent stations and spend time in prayer.

49 Break for Food

During the passing of the peace or the greeting in worship, invite youth to grab a drink and a snack to bring back to their seats for the rest of the worship service. Set up a table off to the side with food and drinks. This allows youth to have ample time to fellowship as part of the worship service.

50 Fill Up With Living Water

When your worship time has a theme of Living Water, give each youth a cup or bottle of water. Whenever the word "water" is said have everyone take a drink of the water and say, "Living Water fills my soul."

Notes

Notes

51 Host an Agape Feast

The love (*agape*) feast is a meal of Christian fellowship that mirrors the meals Jesus shared with his disciples and others throughout his ministry. Fellowship and community are celebrated around the theme of a meal.

The love feast should not be confused with Communion, but is similar in some ways. Hold your love feast around a common table with a full banquet of finger foods in various baskets. Have a common cup or pitcher of juice, lemonade, tea, or other beverage. Distribute the food by passing around the baskets and the pitcher.

While the food is being passed, have volunteers read aloud Scripture passages about meals or banquets (for instance, Luke 9:12-17, Jesus feeds the multitudes; Luke 14:16-24, the parable of the great dinner; or John 6:25-35, Jesus is the bread of life). Sing hymns or praise songs and share testimonies. When everyone has been served, have a time of community prayers. Pray for the needs of your group, the needs of your community, your world, and so on. Open the prayer so that everyone gets a chance to pray. Use this time to celebrate and unify the group.

100 Awesome Ideas for Postmodern Youth

52 The Banquet Table

When you cover Scripture about banquets, hold your worship time around a full spread of goodies and be a living banquet with God as the head of the table.

53 Taste the Salt of the Earth

Read aloud Matthew 5:13 and Revelation 3:15-16. Say: "The Matthew passage seems to suggest that if a believer does nothing to better the world because of his or her beliefs, then his or her existence is futile. This verse coincides with Revelation 3:16 where John offers a description of what the Amen, or the Holy Spirit, might say to the angel of the church of Laodicea: 'Because you are lukewarm I am about to spit you out of my mouth.'"

To underscore the need for disciples to have distinct characteristics, a certain "taste," pass around the bowls of popcorn (first the unsalted, and then the salted variety). Ask the youth to examine their actions for what might make it clear to others that they follow Jesus. Challenge them to add flavor to the lives of those around them, to be salty. Feast on the popcorn—and add salt if necessary.

Notes

Provide a large bowl of unsalted popcorn and a large bowl of salted popcorn. Hide the bowls of popcorn until after the discussion of the Scripture.

Sounds

100 Awesome Ideas for Postmodern Youth

Notes

For additional information about Taizé, visit *www.taizé.fr*.

54 Be Multicultural With Your Music

Praise and worship music is not the only kind of music appropriate for youth worship. Some would argue that hymns are too outdated or too hard to sing, but don't overlook the richness of the tradition and theology in hymns. Expand your musical repertoire in worship. Sing songs from a variety of worship traditions—hymns; praise choruses; songs from the Taizé and Iona communities; songs that come from African, Asian, and Native American traditions among others. Try not to sing the same old songs, but gain new insight into the faith by delving into great music from outside the "norm" of youth worship.

55 Practice Hearing the Word Spoken

When the community gathers for worship, encourage people not to read their Bibles. Rather, encourage the participants to really listen, to truly hear the Scriptures as they are read. Practice with the readers on inflection, tone, and pacing so that the hearers will be free to listen to the words and not be distracted by the speaking.

100 Awesome Ideas for Postmodern Youth

56 Rushing Wind

During Pentecost, set up several fans blowing from every angle in the room. Have a group reading of Acts 2 and emphasize the rushing wind that penetrated the crowd. Sing songs about the Holy Spirit's rushing wind and discuss the feeling of the wind from the fans blowing around the worship space.

You may even want to have prayer stations set up around each fan. For instance, have different prayers that help youth experience the wind of the Spirit at each fan. Encourage them to stand in the way of the breeze and pray the prayers—even linger as they feel the wind on their faces.

If you have a regular worship service for Pentecost, consider setting up fans all around the worship space and leave them running for the service.

57 Listen to Running, Living Water

When you have a service that deals with a Scripture lesson about water, set up running fountains on the altar. Hide some microphones behind the fountains so that the sound of running water will fill the worship space. Project images of water on a screen as a visual to the sound.

Notes

In place of the fountains, you may record the sound of running water or buy a sound-effects tape of a babbling brook or similar sound. Additional sounds you may use are rain, a dripping faucet, and so forth.

Notes

58 Testify

Make the sharing of faith journeys a regular part of the service. Testimonies were a part of early church worship and are routinely included in some traditions today. Allow your group members to grow together as a community of faith by carrying one another's burdens and celebrating the joys of the group.

59 Vary Your Musical Styles

It is vitally important for youth worship to include good music. A number of postmodern worship services across the country produce great music, but not every worship community will enjoy another's worship style. While gathering a group of musicians can sometimes be relatively easy, getting musicians to be unified in purpose and style is quite another thing.

Identify what kind of music defines your specific community and strive to meet that primary need. Then expand that definition by adding various instruments that bring in music from other cultures. Don't worship in a vacuum. Use the vast musical resources from around the world. For instance, have an entire worship time of drumming or another service worshiping with Spanish praise songs.

60 Tongsung Kido (Pray Aloud)

Experience a Korean form of praying in which the worshiping community is praying aloud but individually about a common theme or petition. If you have a particular concern among your community, come together and fill the room with the sounds of your prayers. You could also incorporate this idea for a confirmation or graduation where the community is praying aloud together for each individual.

61 Be Interactive

Sometimes preaching tends to be more about wrestling a text into submission and piecing it out in bite-sized morsels for a community of faith. In the meantime, the community of faith is often left to receive a lecture of how faith ought to be apprehended, experienced, and lived. If the goal of proclamation is transformation, learning, persuasion, and so on, then all these goals are better accomplished through dialogue.

Ask questions. Encourage dialogue and even silent reflection in your message.

Notes

Notes

62 Experience Lectio Divina in Worship

Lectio Divina, spiritual or holy reading, is an ancient discipline of the church practiced by the early church mothers and fathers. Lectio Divina could also be connected to the psalm writers who wrote, "Happy are those who . . . delight . . . in the law of the LORD, and on his law they meditate day and night" (Psalm 1:1-2). The focus is on reading a passage, then waiting in silence to see what the Holy Spirit will illuminate. When used in a worship setting, the Scripture lesson for the service takes on a completely different feel. Instead of hearing the Scripture so that we know where the message is going, we hear the Scriptures and wait for a message from God through the Word.

Before the practice begins, have a youth pray to invite God to come and speak to your group. Have volunteers read the same passage a minimum of three times with extended periods of silence in between. Wait on the Holy Spirit in the silence between the readings. Through lectio divina, the reader is not the only one proclaiming the Scriptures, but the Holy Spirit also speaks them into the hearts of the worshipers. Encourage youth to listen not only with the ear, but also with the heart.

63 Use Sound Effects

When you are dealing with a particular theme or Scripture passage that lends itself to sound effects, use them in the background as you read or during silent meditation. Imagine hearing the sound of the cock crowing as Peter denies Jesus a third time, or the mixture of sounds during Jesus' crucifixion—shouting, hammering, and crowds yelling "Crucify him!" Identify the sound images from your chosen text or theme and add the appropriate sound effects to amplify the experience.

64 Incorporate Popular Music in Worship

Anytime you can connect pop culture to the sacred you will connect a young person with the sacred. Find out what music your youth are listening to and select some songs that are appropriate to be sung in worship, or songs that lend themselves to a message tie-in. Look especially for hip-hop music because this style of music is very much a part of the postmodern culture and the lyrics usually come from the songwriters' real experiences.

Notes

100 Awesome Ideas for Postmodern Youth

Notes

65 Read in Pairs

This activity tones down the pastor-as-expert concept and raises the bar on practicing the doctrine of the priesthood of all believers. Sometimes people who grow up in the church tend to not truly read the Bible for what it says; rather, they tend to read the Bible to affirm what they already believe.

Hand out a sheet of paper with a Scripture passage formatted as text only, without the different verses marked as such. Have people in groups of two (or no more than three) read the passage together and begin to simply observe what's there and what stands out for them. Encourage them to let the passage speak, instead of assuming that it means only one thing.

66 Pray in Unison Voices

The church has a long history of using unison prayer. These prayers are valuable for integrating theological content and sensitivity to context, season, or placement in a service. In a postmodern environment, unison prayers are of, perhaps, even greater value since they are an experiential reminder of the community of faith.

Sometimes unison prayers are left out of youth ministries because they represent what happens in "regular" church. Just keep in mind that this type of prayer is an "out-loud" way to express community in Christ. Invite the participants to write prayers to be read aloud in unison.

67 Be Quiet

Integrate silence into the entire service. In the modern church silence in a worship service meant that something was wrong—someone forgot his or her cue or missed an entrance. However, the discipline of silence has been long practiced in the history of the church of Jesus Christ. In fact, the desert hermits spent most of their life in silence. The Order of St. Benedict still daily celebrate the "Grand Silence" every evening until the conclusion of breakfast the next morning.

Silence is profound in our noisy culture; it is a refuge from the constant bombardment of information that is part of life. During silence, we quiet ourselves to hear the voice of God. Don't be afraid of having extended periods of silence in worship. At first, your group may take a while to settle down and relax in the holy quiet. As the silence becomes more comfortable, your group will have meaningful encounters with God through the stillness.

Notes

Notes

68 Incorporate Readings From Ancient Christians

Readings taken from biographies or letters of the ancient church fathers and mothers can be a reminder of the communion of saints to which the postmodern church belongs. We must keep in mind that we do not worship in a vacuum; instead we worship in community with Jesus-followers around the world as well as those who have died in the faith.

Some of these early writings are relatively difficult in language and in themes. If you include a selection from a writing during the service, try to have a time of interpretation or illumination on the reading. Tell the students something about the saint who wrote it. Then, you're not reading the passage just for the sake of reading; but rather, you are celebrating the saints and capturing their words for today.

69 Expand Your Horizons

Invite another leader from a different church or faith tradition to give a message. The church of Jesus Christ is bigger than one denomination or faith tradition. Yet it is all too rare that different fellowships gather as the unified Body of Christ.

An expression of authentic community is to invite a leader from another church or faith tradition to bring a teaching or have some type of involvement in the worship gathering. It is good for those involved in both fellowships, and it is a valuable example to the spiritual explorers that followers of Jesus can actually love one another (rather than simply point out where others ought to love).

70 Present as a Readers Theatre

Recruit a group of readers to make the Bible lesson a dramatic reading in the style of readers theater. Dramatize the text verbally while still reading the verses word for word. This approach will make the Scripture come alive for the worshipers as they get drawn into the reading. You'll need a narrator and a reader for each character or section of the Scripture lesson.

Notes

Touch

Notes

71 Anoint People With Oil

In ancient times oil was used in medicine for dressing wounds. The church (especially the Eastern Church) adopted this concept and expected that the oil (which had been prayed over) could be used for spiritual healing. The priest baptizes the infant in a font of both water and oil. The sign of the cross is made with the oil on the forehead of an individual who is seeking healing. The Old Testament records the anointing of oil as the method by which a member of the community was set apart for leadership.

Using these practices in a postmodern worship service aligns the community with a historical and biblical practice. Using the practice of anointing also provides another opportunity for a multisensory worship experience.

Look in your denomination's book of worship to find a service of anointing. Then refine the service, if necessary, to meet the needs of your group.

72 Try the Potter's Hand

If possible have a potter come to your worship time and share his or her faith as it relates to molding clay. Give each participant a chance to spin the wheel and touch the wet clay. Then give everyone a small chunk of clay or other malleable substance to hold as a volunteer reads aloud Isaiah 64:8 and Jeremiah18:1-11. Invite the youth to make a symbol with their clay that represents how they see God molding them.

Ask: What is God doing in and through your life? At what times have we resisted the work of the Potter and had to be re-formed on the wheel?

Give the participants a few minutes of silence with their clay to pray about the questions. Then give everyone a chance to talk about what God is saying to him or her through this experience.

Notes

Notes

73 Remember Your Baptism

Whether baptism in your denomination is done by sprinkling infants or plunging believers under the water, all Christians take seriously the call to be baptized. In baptism we confess Jesus Christ as Lord and make an outward commitment both to Christian living and to Christian community. Help the youth continually reflect on their baptism and what it means as they mature in faith. Teach them that while the act of baptism is a one-time thing, the work of the Spirit is ongoing.

Have a service to remember one's baptism by gathering together around some water and reading together Matthew 3 in its entirety. Then silently meditate on the ways in which the worshipers are living out their baptism. Talk about baptism as an ongoing work of the Spirit—as living out the covenant made in baptism. Take a tree branch full of leaves and dip it into the water. Then shake the branch around your worship space so that each youth feels the water fall on him or her. As you do this say, "Remember your baptism, be thankful, and live fully empowered by the Holy Spirit. Amen." Encourage the youth to splash water onto their faces regularly and say to themselves, "I belong to God" as an act of remembering their baptism.

74 Stand on the Rock

Find the largest rock possible to set in your worship space; or experience this worship idea outside around a large boulder, hill, mountain, or other rock formation. Also mark off a section with different items to be walked on that will make the ground "shaky" (sand, mud, loose gravel, a tightrope, and so on).

Have the participants take off their shoes and walk on the "shaky ground." After all have had a chance, discuss the ways in which our lives can be shaky and the instability of walking on our own through life. Then have a volunteer read aloud Psalm 40:1-3. Invite volunteers to tell about times when they experienced God as the Rock on which they stand. Then have everyone find a place to stand on the rock, either one at a time or all together, and recite the psalm again. Encourage the youth to stand on our Rock so that others will put their trust in the Lord also.

Notes

Notes

7 5 Wade in the Water

When you're on a retreat or camping trip, have your worship time knee deep in the lake or swimming pool. Various themes work for this experience: crossing the Jordan River, being streams in the desert, walking out to Jesus, and so forth.

7 6 Touch the Cross

Sometime during Lent, gather around a wooden cross as you tell the story of the Crucifixion. Have a prayer time that gives youth a chance to feel the cross as they pray. If you incorporate this idea for an indoor service, lean the cross against the altar table and drape colored cloth over it. Surround the cross with tea light candles as the only light in the room.

Often the cross in the worship space is far removed from the congregation. For this worship experience, allow the youth to be as close to the cross as possible to give them an added sense of awe in prayer.

77 Give Us Clean Hands

Have a hand-washing service as you sing together "Give Us Clean Hands" and study Psalm 24:1-6. Place a bowl of water on the altar with several towels. Ask a volunteer to read aloud the psalm and then sing the praise song a few times. As the music continues, give a brief message about the psalm and the challenge to stand holy before God. Have some silent time as the youth reflect on the cleanliness of their hands and the purity of their hearts.

After a few minutes, invite the participants to come to the altar in pairs and wash each other's hands and then kneel in prayer as the hand-washing takes place. When everyone is finished, stand and sing the above song a few more times. Close with a benediction that God will empower your group to be a generation that seeks God first.

Notes

Notes

7 8 Make Symbols in the Sand

Have a large pit of sand for this idea, or gather around an outdoor sandpit. Or provide small bags of sand for each participant. Read from John 8 the story of Jesus and the woman caught in adultery. Explain that the story is usually told to convey our common guilt and that no one is less sinful than another. However, commentaries suggest that this story is more about Jesus' reaction and response to the Pharisees and religious authorities. Jesus would not let the scribes exert power over him or the woman; instead he treated them as equals. His writing in the sand indicated his unwillingness to give the religious authorities the attention they were seeking, or to give credence to their little "test."

Use this story to help the youth examine the subject of religious authority. How do we know when to respect or defy authority? Jesus' symbols in the sand were a sign of his defiance of the pious and corrupt religious leaders. Talk with the participants about situations in which persons in authority have been misleading, corrupt, and/or hateful. Help the youth think about what their "symbols in the sand" or response will be when they find themselves opposed to the teaching of an authority. Will they look down or away? walk away? listen but not act upon the situation? challenge the teaching?

Have the youth play with the sand for a moment. Encourage them to think about situations they have been a part of in which they have disagreed with someone in authority, or someone who has tried to "test" them. Pray for the courage to speak the truth and be a prophetic voice in the world today.

79 Walk on Water

Gather around a shallow pool and let everyone soak his or her feet in the water. Talk about Jesus walking on water and let the participants walk across the shallow water imagining that they are floating atop the surface. As the youth are seated around the pool, invite them to let their feet skim the top of the water. Discuss what the water feels like as it touches only the bottoms of their feet. Have a time of prayer to pray for God's assurance and guidance as we walk through the storms in life.

Notes

Notes

80 Wash One Another's Feet

In the time of the Scripture writers, people walked on foot to get where they were going. They literally carried their burdens on their feet. Recall the many references to washing feet in Scripture, from Genesis to the New Testament. This act symbolized servanthood, hospitality, and friendship. Take time as a community to wash one another's feet and reflect on any one of the passages in the Bible that speak of the ritual.

A variation on this act is the giving of back rubs. Our feet do not necessarily carry our stresses and burdens these days; instead we feel stress in the back and neck areas. Liken the practice of foot washing to caring for one another by rubbing the shoulders of a friend.

81 Hold Hands to Close

During your benediction or closing act of worship, gather in a circle and instruct the youth to cross their right hand over their left hand and join both hands to their neighbors' hands. When the blessing is finished, have the participants raise their hands over their heads, turn outward, and declare, "Amen!"

82 Worship by Campfire

You have probably had a worship time or two as a youth group around a campfire. Whether you are at camp or at your church you can still capture the same feeling and warmth of the heat from the fire. Get a hold of an outdoor fireplace and have a worship service on your church lawn. (Of course, you will need to have a few buckets of water handy.) Spread blankets around the fireplace and pretend that you're camping and celebrating your community. Feel the warmth from the fire, the freshness of the ground, and the sense of communion with one another.

83 Drum Your Prayers

Celebrate the tradition of drumming in your worship time by gathering drums of various sizes. Try to have a drum for each person. You will pray in silence and let the sound of the drums represent your prayers rising to God. Invite one person to begin with a drumbeat and then have others join in one by one as they are ready to pray. The sound can easily move one to tears and the youth will have a prayer experience like no other.

Notes

6

Movement

Worship feast Worship feast Worship fe

Notes

84 Use a Labyrinth

This ancient practice is a contemplative exercise that involves walking through a maze in order to center on Christ. A labyrinth outlined on the floor presents a vivid image that can enhance the environment of worship. Even if a person doesn't walk through the labyrinth, it is a valuable tool for contemplation. A simple element like masking tape on carpet can create the desired effect. If meeting outside, use sand, chalk, bricks, or small stones. If possible, involve members of the community in creating the labyrinth.

This activity is especially appropriate during special seasons such as Lent or Advent. The labyrinth is intended to be a place where one focuses on prayer. As the participants walk the maze-like pattern, they should allow themselves to focus solely on listening for God's still small voice. Once the worshipers have made it to the center of the labyrinth, they are to sit quietly and listen for what God might be saying through the Scripture. As each person exits the circle, he or she is to focus on what God is calling him or her to do in the world and how to go about living differently.

85 Have a Gathering of Prayer

The early church viewed prayer as a significant activity for the gathered community of faith. The community seemed to always be together praying when something occurred in the early parts of the Book of Acts. Yet, often in our contexts of worship, prayer is simply an introduction or conclusion to an important element. Worse, prayer can be used simply as a transition.

A service of prayer recalls the importance of prayer in the community. Provide a greeter/interpreter for those who arrive and are expecting a different type of service. Have the worshipers enter a dark room where many candles are already lit, images are scrolling on the screen, and a CD of chant music is playing. Have no chairs in the room, only rugs and pillows in a semicircle. Hand out various historical quotations, prayers, and Scriptures as a guide for this hour-long silent prayer time.

After your first prayer meeting, you may want to debrief the experience with the youth. Invite them to talk about what they felt or didn't feel, or how they became closer to God.

Notes

Notes

86 Move to Receive Communion

Jesus told his disciples to "do this in remembrance of me." The term *remembrance* represents more than a simple, cognitive event. It is an experiential review of God's faithfulness to the people of the covenant from Abraham to us. All the biblical texts and many liturgies include an offering of the elements of the Lord's Supper at the table. Oftentimes the pastor says, "Come to the table"; but the leaders of the church get up and serve the people seated in pews little glasses of grape juice with a morsel of cracker or bread.

Invite people to the table and let them be served there at the altar. Help the youth sense the full mystery of the event by kneeling around the table to receive the body and blood of our Lord.

87 Have Individuals From the Community Bring the Communion Elements

Communion is often the realm of the clergy. In some faith traditions this is the only appropriate way for the Lord's table to have theological value. However, if tradition allows, have individuals or groups purchase or make bread and juice.

Consider having the women's group in the church bake bread for youth group Communion or having some members of the youth group make juice using a homemade juicer.

Having the elements come from the community is a way to adhere to the practice of the earliest church fellowships that met in people's homes. It is also a way for individuals in the community to practice hospitality for the whole community.

Notes

Notes

88 Make an Altar Call

We surely all have memories of the last night at church camp when we experienced a call to repentance and came forward in tears to the altar. While this moment is fine and good, the altar is not only a place for an emotional response to an exciting message. The altar is where we lay our lives before the Lord, where we intercede for those who need our prayers, where we commit to following Jesus, and where we simply spend time in conversation with God.

Create an altar or kneeling rail in your worship space and encourage the youth to linger there during worship prayer times. Have your community prayers, your mission trip commissioning, your silent prayer time, and other times special to your group around the altar. Make this place a "home" for the personal prayer times of your youth.

89 Receive an Offering

Don't limit the group's understanding of "offering" to simply money. Have a time of offering in worship where the participants can share their gifts and talents as a gift both to the community and to God. That said, don't forget that most youth do have some money of their own through working, babysitting, or getting an allowance. Encourage them to begin tithing and giving monetary offerings.

When it comes to the church and money, the Western church has suffered at the hands of televangelists who have abused the call of Christ to offer our money along with our lives. However, this fact does not negate the call to give God a portion of our income and other physical gifts. Make the time for offering a dynamic experience in worship. While it is sometimes appropriate to pass the plate during the worship service, it can be equally appropriate to have a passive offering where people can participate in the offering on their way out of the worship gathering. Another way to approach the offering is to have an offering plate up-front-and-center where the worshipers physically walk to the altar and place a gift in the plate.

Notes

Notes

90 Have a Progressive Worship Experience

Start at one location and travel to different areas as you move through different parts of the service. End at someone's home with the celebration of Communion. One excellent idea is to plan the worship experience around the pattern of worship outlined in *The Book of Common Prayer* (see "An Order for Celebrating the Holy Eucharist"). Consider holding each segment of the worship in a different home. For instance:

Home 1: "Gathering": Everyone meets at the first home and words of welcome and directions for the evening are discussed.

Home 2: "Proclaim and Respond to God's Word": A devotional is shared with the group, along with singing, dance, other art forms, and silent prayer.

Home 3: "Prayer and Peace": Upon entering the home everyone receives a candle and sits in a circle formation. The leader lights his or her candle and begins sharing personal prayer concerns. Then the leader lights the candle of the next person and the cycle continues around the circle. Once everyone has spoken, have a time of silence. End with passing the peace.

100 Awesome Ideas for Postmodern Youth

Home 4: "Prepare the Table": At this home you actually bake your own bread, go to the fridge and find your juice, gather glasses (make sure that you supply the home with enough glasses beforehand and with any items that are needed to decorate your worship space).

Home 5: "Breaking Bread and Sharing the Gifts of God": When you arrive at the last home for the night, the youth find that it happens to be the senior pastor's. He or she welcomes the group into the house and together you all create your worship space. The pastor then proceeds to retell the Communion story and blesses the sacraments and everyone takes Communion together. Afterward, there is singing and a closing prayer.

91 Get Outside Yourself

Go to several different denominations' churches, such as Pentecostal, Eastern Orthodox, Baptist, United Methodist, and so forth. Choose churches that have very different worship styles—contemporary, traditional, charismatic, contemplative. Then have the youth discuss what they enjoyed about each style and plan a service using elements of each one.

Notes

100 Awesome Ideas for Postmodern Youth

Notes

92 Have a Formal Dinner Party

Invite the youth to dress up in formal attire. Instead of a meal serve Holy Communion. Build the worship experience around the theme of "God's banquet." Play light jazz or piano music in the background. Youth will enjoy seeing one another dressed so nicely. They will be anticipating a fine meal but will not be sure what to expect during the evening.

The sound of a glass rings and everyone quiets as they anticipate someone beginning a toast. The toast begins with familiar words that they recall hearing before—retelling of Jesus sharing a meal with his disciples. As the Communion story is told, "waiters" bring out dishes with bread and juice. Everyone takes Holy Communion together and tells some of their favorite experiences with family and friends that involve sharing a meal, meanwhile the "waiters" return with a nice meal for all to enjoy together.

93 Visit the Wilderness

During Lent, take the participants to a nearby state park and have your worship experience in the middle of the forest and focus on "being in the wilderness" of our lives.

94 Focus On God as Creator and Mystery

Take your group to a waterfall where they can experience nature and the wonder of God. Talk about the ever-flowing stream of God's love and the mystery of a waterfall that runs seemingly on its own, but silently prompted by God.

95 Host a Scavenger Hunt Worship Experience

Send the participants in teams all over the area on a scavenger hunt that focuses on a certain theme. End up in one central location where you will have a closing worship that is based around your theme.

96 Host a Rave Worship Service

Follow a very liturgical pattern for worship but create a "club" atmosphere using darkness, black lights, strobe lights, Christian chant music with an added beat, and dancing. Have Holy Communion as the central element of the service.

Notes

Notes

97 Follow the Stations of the Cross

Set up fourteen small wooden crosses in your worship space or on your church yard. Make a handout with the following information and let your youth walk to each cross to pray and meditate.

1. Jesus before Pilate (Matthew 27:11-31)
   Pray that others would know that you are a Christian by your life.

2. Jesus takes up his cross (John 19:17)
   Pray that you would have the courage to take up your cross and follow Jesus.

3. Jesus falls.
   Pray that you would walk tall and not stumble in your faith.

4. Jesus seeks care for his mother (John 19:25-27)
   Pray for your family.

5. Simon carries Jesus' cross (Mark 15:21)
   Pray for the strength to support others.

6. Jesus' face is wiped.
   Pray for the courage to be kind.

100 Awesome Ideas for Postmodern Youth

7. Jesus falls again.
   Pray for those who cause you to stumble.

8. Women weep for Jesus (Luke 23:27)
   Pray for those who may be grieving.

9. Jesus falls again.
   Pray for power to stand against injustice.

10. Jesus' clothes are stripped (John 19:23-25)
    Pray for those who have been violated in
    this world.

11. Jesus is nailed to the cross (Mark 15:37)
    Praise Christ for taking your place.

12. Jesus dies (Mark 15:37)
    Pray for the hope that only God can give.

13. Jesus is taken off the cross
    (Luke 23:50-53)
    Pray for the courage to live for Christ.

14. Jesus is buried (John 19:38)
    Pray that you would live
    your faith actively and
    abundantly in the world.

Notes

Notes

98 Stand Up, Sit Down

Sometimes in worship we take the standing and sitting in worship for granted. Some stand for the reading of the Gospel books, others stand for any Scripture reading, still others don't stand at all for the reading of Scriptures. We stand in worship to let our bodies participate in the experience; we also "stand in the need of prayer."

Don't assume that the motion of standing and sitting is irrelevant, or that young persons don't like the repetition of it. Talk with your group about appropriate times to stand in worship and those times when sitting or kneeling is more meaningful. Then put your discussion into action in worship. This way the youth know why they stand or sit and they find meaning in the motion.

99 Interview Teens at School

Assign a group of youth a topic related to the theme of worship experiences. Send the participants out to interview and videotape teens at their school talking about this theme. Show the videotape as part of the worship.

100 Slouch if You Want To

What posture should a person assume while he or she worships God? Peruse the Psalms and find a multiplicity of mannerisms:

Psalm 5:7—"But I, by your great mercy, will come into your house; in reverence will I bow down toward your holy temple."

Psalm 63:—"I will bless you as long as I live; I will lift up my hands."

There is no one right way to posture oneself physically before the Lord. Some worshipers find the freedom to express their worship by lying prostrate before a cross. Others choose to stand with arms lifted high. Because there are multiple postures for worship, the worship leaders should encourage those gathered to authentically express themselves before God in worship.

Notes

Multimedia Resources

iworship: a total worship experience
This is an amazing worship tool for multisensory worship. A two-disc CD contains 33 popular worship songs. Complete song tracks and a CD-ROM enhanced songbook are available as well as a DVD component with lyrics set on beautiful images. iworship is a total multimedia worship experience that combines the latest advances in audiovisual presentations with the most powerful songs in the church today. The multimedia resource combines powerful worship songs with audiovisual presentations to make your worship a holy experience. To purchase visit *iworshipnow.com*.

The Faith We Sing (Pew Edition, Cross Only Cover) (ISBN 0-68704-904-0)
This songbook is rich in global praise music, new hymns, Taizé and Iona chants, and popular praise songs. Nowhere else will you find the rich combination of music in one resource. Also available in a Guitar Edition, a MIDI Edition, a Presentation Edition, and a CD-ROM Edition. Visit *www.thefaithwesing.com*; order this resource at *www.cokesbury.com*.

Verticallife: A Youth Ministry Worship Resource (Version 2.1)
Verticallife is a subscription service. Each issue includes a demonstration CD with 10 popular modern worship songs, accompaniment tracks on CD, PowerPoint® compatible lyrics, transparency masters with lyrics, chord charts and rhythm charts, and MediaShout® media—for ministry presentation software. This resource will keep you up to date with the latest worship music and equip you, your leaders, and musicians. Learn more about the resource and subscribe at *verticallife.com*.

Songbooks

Songs for Taizé (ISBN 2-85040-128-5)
For a deeper prayer and meditative experience in worship, familiarize yourself with the tradition of Taizé prayer services. The songs are sung repetitively so as to begin to live and breathe the prayers. Learn more about Taizé at *www.taizé.fr*.

Passion Songbook (ISBN 3-47401-296-7)
This new compilation songbook features every song recorded on all four Passion projects. It contains sheet music for the piano and guitar, chord sheets for guitar, and overhead masters for congregational/Bible study use.

Compact Discs

David Crowder Band—*Can You Hear Us?* (ASIN: B000060NV3)

Charlie Hall—*Porch and Altar* (ASIN: 0724385182426)

Passion Worship Band—Passion: *OneDay Live* (ASIN: B00004ZDMT)

Passion Worship Band—*The Road to OneDay* (ASIN: B00004R96A)

Passion Worship Band—Passion: *Our Love Is Loud: Live* (ASIN: B000063RST)

Passion Worship Band—*Better Is OneDay* (ASIN: B00000ILYJ)

Passion '98: *Live Worship From the 268 Generation: Live* (ASIN: B000007SEP)

Michael W. Smith—*Worship* (ASIN: B00005NQJV)

Chris Tomlin—*Not to Us* (ASIN: B00006I0CK)

Chris Tomlin—*The Noise We Make* (ASIN: 5551044076)

Websites

worshiptogether.com
This website will keep you current on the worship scene with the latest songs from today's most popular worship leaders. Buy CDs, songbooks, chord charts, and more.

arttoheartweb.com/worship_resources.htm
Learn how to use classical paintings in worship and find out more about worship styles and resources.

www.sacramentis.com
Look for poetry, graphics, and articles about postmodern worship.

www.theooze.com
Find a listing of links to churches in your state meeting the worshiping needs of postmodern youth.

www.emergentvillage.com
Join a community of church leaders who are studying and anticipating cultural shifts and how those shifts play out in the church.